Complex Sales

T0335090

Ken Langdon

- ■ Fast-track route to beating the competition and successfully closing complex sales

- ■ Covers getting to grips with the technical and commercial risks that make up complex selling, understanding the needs of the buyer, effectively managing the time and resource spent in carrying out a complex sale, and implementing a successful sales campaign

- ■ Worked example of a team-built sales campaign plan

- ■ Includes a comprehensive resources guide, key concepts and thinkers, a 10-step action plan to winning complex sales, and a section of FAQs

≫EXPRESS EXEC.COM≪
essential management thinking at your fingertips

SALES

12.04

The right of Ken Langdon to be identified as the author of this book has been asserted in accordance with the Copyright, Designs and Patents Act 1988

First Published 2003 by
Capstone Publishing Limited (a Wiley company)
8 Newtec Place
Magdalen Road
Oxford OX4 1RE
United Kingdom
http://www.capstoneideas.com

CIP catalogue records for this book are available from the British Library and the US Library of Congress

ISBN 1-84112-457-5

Wiley also publishes its books in a variety of electronic formats. Some content that appears in print may not be available in electronic books.

Websites often change their contents and addresses; details of sites listed in this book were accurate at the time of writing, but may change.

Substantial discounts on bulk quantities of Capstone Books are available to corporations, professional associations and other organizations. For details telephone Capstone Publishing on (+44-1865-798623), fax (+44-1865-240941) or email (info@wiley-capstone.co.uk).

FSC
Mixed Sources
Product group from well-managed
forests and other controlled sources

Cert no. SGS-COC-2953
www.fsc.org
© 1996 Forest Stewardship Council

Contents

Introduction to ExpressExec

ExpressExec is a completely up-to-date resource of current business practice, accessible in a number of ways – anytime, anyplace, anywhere. ExpressExec combines best practice cases, key ideas, action points, glossaries, further reading, and resources.

Each module contains 10 individual titles that cover all the key aspects of global business practice. Written by leading experts in their field, the knowledge imparted provides executives with the tools and skills to increase their personal and business effectiveness, benefiting both employee and employer.

ExpressExec is available in a number of formats:

» **Print** – 120 titles available through retailers or printed on demand using any combination of the 1200 chapters available.
» **E-Books** – e-books can be individually downloaded from ExpressExec.com or online retailers onto PCs, handheld computers, and e-readers.
» **Online** – http://www.expressexec.wiley.com/ provides fully searchable access to the complete ExpressExec resource via the Internet – a cost-effective online tool to increase business expertise across a whole organization.

» **ExpressExec Performance Support Solution (EEPSS)** – a software solution that integrates ExpressExec content with interactive tools to provide organizations with a complete internal management development solution.

» **ExpressExec Rights and Syndication** – ExpressExec content can be licensed for translation or display within intranets or on Internet sites.

To find out more visit www.ExpressExec.com or contact elound@wiley-capstone.co.uk.

Introduction to Complex Sales

This chapter considers why complex sales need:

» high and wide levels of contact within the prospective customer;
» a team approach; and
» a well thought-out sales strategy and action plan.

Many organizations are involved in complex sales. These are sales campaigns where a number of people are involved on the selling and buying sides. They are campaigns with strategic value to the customer. A complex sale means that a prospect is being asked to go ahead with a project where there are technical and commercial risks, and where the potential benefits to the prospect may be very large indeed.

You will find complex sales in many different industries. A banking organization proposing a reappraisal of the banking facilities used by a multinational corporation; a software company selling a new application to a medium-sized business; a building industry consulting company using a team of subcontractors to bid for a major project – all of these can use the processes of professional complex sales planning.

» **Complex sales fact one** – very few competitive sales plans are lost because the selling team did not understand enough about its own products and services, but many complex sales are lost because the selling team did not understand enough about the customer and its problems and opportunities and about what the selling team's products and services would do to benefit them.
» **Complex sales fact two** – very few sales campaigns are lost because the selling team was talking and selling to too many people in the prospect's organization, but many complex sales are lost because of activity within the prospect that was unknown to the selling team.
» **Complex sales fact three** – it is not possible for selling teams to find out too early in the campaign that there is not enough benefit for the customer to go ahead with the complex project, but it is quite possible for a selling team to spend time and resources in continuing a campaign after the point where it has become obvious to someone in the prospect organization that the proposal cannot go ahead.

Now for the "so-what" test. This is a good mantra for a professional seller to check that what they are proposing has real relevance to a selling situation. It is at its best when being used in the context of a brilliant feature of a product or service, as in the following example.

» "Our system has got a broadband access mechanism" – "So what?"
» "It means that our system can handle up to 200 calls per hour" – "So what?"

» "If your requirement rises from its current 50 calls per hour by as much as four times, you will not need to invest any more money in telecommunications equipment" – "Ah, now I see." At last the salesperson has got to the real customer benefit – the impact of the feature on the profitability of the prospect.

If the above facts about complex sales are correct, so what? First of all, they are all lessons learnt by professional salespeople who have lost complex sales campaigns either because the prospect decided in the end to do nothing or because the selling team lost to a competitor.

What can you do to avoid the pitfalls of these facts and to make sure that complex sales campaigns are successful? Sell high and wide – find out all of the key people, or stakeholders, in both the selling and buying organizations and work out their attitudes and preferences. Work as a team – make sure that everyone involved is aware of the sales strategy and has agreed to their role in it.

Above all, establish and implement a professional sales campaign plan. The processes for qualifying the prospect and working on changing the attitudes of the key people where necessary are looked at in the following chapters. Use them and you will win more complex sales campaigns, beat the competition more frequently, and make more profit.

What is Meant

by Complex Sales?

This chapter looks at the following key phrases:

- » solution selling;
- » planning a complex sales campaign;
- » qualifying the prospect; and
- » teams and virtual teams.

SOLUTION SELLING

The key characteristic of complex sales campaigns is seen primarily in the involvement of the selling team with the customer's business. The team needs to understand the impact of the products under consideration on the actual financial results and image of the prospect.

In high-technology, for example, such a sales campaign would be an opportunity, probably in competition, to supply products and services that will enable the customer to do things differently. It may be a multimillion-pound deal or it may be a small project of great strategic importance to the customer. In either case, the seller needs to understand enough about the customer's business to be able to couch the proposal in the customer's terms and identify and agree the financial and other benefits of the project.

With fast-moving consumer goods (FMCG), the example may be related to a particular promotion to which the seller wishes the customer to apply resources in terms of people and money – it may be using combinations of marketing information to extend markets and market-share.

This type of business-oriented selling is known as "solution selling" as opposed to product-based selling. To engage in solution selling we need to examine two key questions: how salespeople gather the information they need to produce an effective solution-selling campaign; and how the selling team martials its resources to establish a persuasive business argument for the sale and sells it to the customer.

The objectives of solution selling are:

» to make a competitive sale by working with the customer to understand the return on investment offered by your products and services;
» to produce satisfied customers;
» to gain a competitive edge by recognizing earlier than your competitors where the customer should invest next; and
» to build customer loyalty by improving the performance of the customer and giving no reason for them to look elsewhere.

If a franking machine salesperson has the Empire State Building as their patch, it is of such a size that it is going to be difficult for the salesperson to understand the business benefits that his machines are giving to each of the customers. They do not buy one if they do not need one. Beyond that, it is not the job of the product-seller to help the customer understand the differences that using the machine is going to have on the bottom line of the business.

Solution selling is different. The salesperson is working on the premise that a customer who understands what a product or service is actually achieving for the business is the sort of customer who buys more of that product or service. The aim of solution selling becomes not just to make profits for the seller, but also to make profits for the buyer.

An account manager who was selling computer systems to a major telephone company struggled with this concept. He found it "intellectually dishonest" to take as a campaign objective one that had to do with the health of the buyer as opposed to the profits of the seller. The customer called halt at one point, did an audit of all computer systems and discovered that he had more than enough and that some were simply not paying their way. That same account manager was then thrown onto the defensive, trying to justify after the event the purchases that the customer had made.

THE CAMPAIGN PLAN'S THE THING

In the end, an agreed approach to all aspects of selling and customer care emerges as the result of a plan, and a plan emerges as a result of understanding the current situation, agreeing the desired outcomes, agreeing the actions needed to complete a successful campaign, allocating resources and timescales to those actions, and monitoring the implementation of the plan.

Notice how these principles speak in terms of "agreeing" – complex sales plans are the result of all the stakeholders agreeing with the sales strategy and taking accountability for the actions allocated to them. So, we define the desired outcomes of the plan as the "objectives," and how the team is going to achieve those objectives as the "sales strategy."

One more word needs to be added to the definition of the sales strategy – it must be a "competitive" or "winning" sales strategy. This brings in the hugely important attribute of a campaign plan – its differentiators. A winning sales strategy answers the question, "Why is the customer going to buy from us rather than from one of our competitors?"

QUESTION: WHEN IS A PROSPECT FULLY QUALIFIED?

Answer: when the order is signed by the customer and countersigned by the seller. Qualification is the process of checking how likely it is that the customer is going to buy from us, and the process of qualification therefore never ends. It is the answer to the qualification checklist that guides the selling team on what needs to be done. For the purposes of definition, take just one of the questions in the qualification template: "Are all the key people positive about going ahead with us?"

At the beginning of the campaign we will attempt, and probably succeed, in identifying which personnel from our and the customer's side will be involved in the decision process and what their roles will be. But these things never stand still. People move around within organizations, and other people come into the buying company from other organizations and possibly hold different views on the subject. The qualification process has to include keeping the list of key people up to date and feeding into the action plan any changes in those people or in their attitudes towards us.

It is very difficult for a selling team to be faced, for example, with a senior member of the customer's organization becoming involved with a campaign late in the selling-and-buying cycle, as such a person could bring a different viewpoint which is not necessarily advantageous to the selling team's position. A good example of this is if the managing director comes into the process late. They may well take the word of their technical recommenders that the products being proposed will do the job. They will almost certainly take the word of their financial people if they say that the project is financially viable, but they may also add their own dimension – "That is all very well, but can we make it work in this organization at this time? Is the implementation plan a practical one that I can monitor? We do not want another project or management initiative that starts off with a flourish but never makes it through to the predicted conclusion."

Forewarned is forearmed in these circumstances – knowing the propensity of managing directors to act in this way means that we can make sure that a practical implementation plan exists even if no one in the early stages of the campaign has insisted on one. It is a good illustration of the fact that the qualifying process does not stop until the ink is dry on the contract.

TEAMS AND VIRTUAL TEAMS

A key attribute of the good salesperson is the ability to use purely charismatic power to motivate people to achieve their part in the salesperson's plan for a complex sale. Normal practice has the salesperson responsible only for the performance of the company in a particular campaign, without them being responsible for the "pay and rations" of the marketing and supporting of people involved in the campaign.

The salesperson for an advertising agency pitching for the Proctor & Gamble account worldwide might have 10 or more people working in sales, support, and creative roles, with each possibly working for a different line-manager. This gives an idea of the complexity of implementing a plan without having direct control over the necessary resources.

Add in the factor that the Proctor & Gamble account is live on five continents and in 150 countries, and the problem looks formidable. It *is* formidable, and the supervision and motivation of "virtual teams" needs attention not just in terms of business processes but also in terms of the skills involved in the management of people through leadership and motivation.

So far we have looked at the implementation teams working on the products and services being supplied. We probably need to take into account the senior management teams in both the selling and buying organizations. Frequently, the situation arises where a high-achiever salesperson has become a senior manager in the supplying firm. This poses new problems. The customer's people will probably want to continue to deal with the person they know, despite the fact they have moved into other roles. Professional salespeople need diplomacy as well as business processes to deal with a situation involving egos as well as business logic.

KEY LEARNING POINTS

» The key difference between a product salesperson and one who deals in consultative complex sales campaigns is the care with which the salesperson identifies the prospect's business problems and opportunities.
» The fact that complex sales requires a team on the seller's side emphasizes the need for an agreed strategy and sales plan so that everyone is concentrating their efforts on the strategy that the salesperson believes will win the business.

The Evolution of Complex Sales

This chapter looks at the evolution, through trial and error over the years, of current thinking about complex sales planning in terms of:

» the first company to be renowned for doing it; and
» the driver of the campaign – the customer's buying process.

IBM AND THE ORIGIN OF SOLUTION SELLING

Many people think that Thomas Watson Sr built IBM into a big computer company and that he was a captain of industry. But in fact it was his son, Thomas Watson Jr, who did this after he moved into the company's top management at the age of 32. It was he who transformed IBM from a medium-sized company into an industrial giant.

But it was Watson Sr who, one could say, invented complex sales planning. He was set on building a company that would become larger and more successful than National Cash Register (NCR), the company for which he worked as a young man. Indeed, his success was built around many of the lessons he had learned at NCR.

He leased rather than sold machines and insisted that customers used only his company's punched cards. But selling was deemed all-important and Watson went to great lengths to elevate the status of his sales teams, saying: "I want my IBM salesmen to be people to whom their wives and their children look up. I don't want their mothers to feel that they have to apologize for them or have to dissimulate when they are being asked what their son is doing."[1]

The five IBM business goals that spawned complex sales planning were:

» to enhance customer partnerships;
» to be the leader in products and services, excelling in quality and innovation;
» to grow with the industry;
» to be the most efficient in everything we do; and
» to sustain our profitability, which funds our growth.

This striving for excellence and creating customer partnerships is the starting point of solution selling from the seller's point of view. The other concept which has driven solution selling is, of course, the buyer's point of view. We will take as an example the most complex buying decisions that customers make – the purchasing and exploiting of capital assets in terms of plant and machinery.

MEETING CUSTOMER NEEDS – HOW DOES A COMPANY DECIDE WHAT PROJECTS TO INVEST IN?

The driver of any sales campaign has to be the customer. Until the sales team understands the political, financial, and technical considerations which go into a buying decision, it cannot plan how to meet customer needs.

At any point in time, a company is being offered, by its managers and by outsiders, many more ideas than it can afford to implement. There is constant pressure in terms of requests for allocation of funds from product development managers, designers, information technology groups, and others throughout the business. This causes most companies to develop management processes for investment appraisal and project management.

To understand this process we need to follow the sensible company's step-by-step guide to capital investment appraisal and implementation, set out below.

» Establish the objectives of the project within the company's business strategy.
» Involve the management and staff who will have their jobs changed as a result of the project.
» Agree the tactical business case, including the cost justification.
» Establish implementation priorities and controls.
» Select the exact functionality.
» Select the necessary products and services and their suppliers.
» Implement the project and train the users.
» Evaluate the results and adapt the project for improvement.

Each of the above contains lessons for the solution-seller and requires some further explanation.

Taking the example of an IT project, how do these phases go? While we will assume a series of events, it should be remembered that in reality the implementation is much more complex and that many other things are happening in parallel. Nevertheless, it is useful to examine the process step by step.

Establish the objectives of the project within the company's business strategy

Many IT projects have as their starting point a strategic objective of the company. Indeed, if you look at the way banks have implemented their IT systems, you will find that they have followed the rule of maintaining competitiveness by keeping abreast of new technology developments. From the seller's point of view this "me too" strategy is a fortuitous starting point. It is likely, however, that the strategic reasons for buying will not be sufficient on their own, and managers will have to back them up with a solid business case. It is also important that IT implementations support the key business strategies, such as product or marketing strategies. This is the first hurdle over which any proposal must jump.

Sometimes, strategic considerations will easily transform into a business case, but sometimes the link is more difficult. Consider these three statements from the annual report of a retailer:

» "building a powerful brand around a total fashion approach";
» "we aim to increase profits through the tighter management of stock and a substantial reduction in markdowns"; and
» "our supplier base is now very focused and works closely with us."

If professional salespeople are going to focus a sales campaign on this retailer, they must understand the reality behind these statements and build them into the business case for investment. In other words, sellers must *connect* the benefits of the products they are selling to these high level policies.

The second of the above statements is the easiest to back up with a cost-benefit case. It will therefore have powerful appeal to middle managers and the finance department. Also, senior management may regard any project's contribution to the first statement as being a key motivator.

Involve the management and staff who will have their jobs changed as a result of the project

The only certainty about an IT implementation is that the jobs of some people are going to change. Most large organizations are getting better at managing such change. There are, however, still some, along with many smaller businesses, who handle this part of the process at best insufficiently and at worst insensitively. This imperils the success of the project. Do not confuse this stage with training – it is helping the people involved to understand the benefits of the change to their organization, their customers, and themselves.

Agree the tactical business case, including the cost justification

In almost all organizations there is a standard method of making a business case, and it is vital that the account manager knows what that process is. How close the customer allows you to get to applying that process depends on your relationship and how much value the customer believes you can add to the process.

Here is an example of this part of the process impeding a poor sales approach. I was involved in the case of a bottle manufacturer who wanted to investigate the automation of the hot end of the bottle manufacturing line. In simple terms, machines manufacture the bottles at the hot end of the process. In manual systems, people do the quality checks when the bottle reaches the cold end. If you put automatic instrumentation into the hot end you can detect mis-shapes or other sub-quality product at an earlier stage in the process. Operators can make adjustments to the controls of temperature and pressure earlier, and the number of top quality bottles produced rises significantly. Since you are improving the output of a process, the benefit goes straight through to the profit line. The return on investment is huge, with the payback period as short as a year.

The bottle company consulted potential suppliers of equipment and invited them to tender. They did not invite them to take any part in the financial evaluation. The failure of the salesperson to change this had a marked effect on the eventual profitability and quality of the deal.

A key issue in the tender was maintenance and reliability. The instruments went into a manufacturing process which was continuous. This meant that any failure of the instruments would cause the factory to cease production or to produce a high number of defective products (rejects). During the tender, the suppliers strove to outdo each other, with guaranteed call-out times, resident engineers, and other means of satisfying the concerns of the customer. At the same time, of course, they were lowering the profitability of the deal, and raising the strain on maintenance engineering to perform to contract and to customer expectation. Anyway, a winner emerged and the contract was awarded.

The business case which the customer prepared was an overwhelming one. It basically promised payback in six months and very large additions to the bottom line due to increased efficiency of the new process. The question subsequently arose: "Why did the customer not buy two systems to give fallback reliability?" When asked, the customer's technicians agreed that the thought had crossed their minds, but since the competing suppliers had not suggested it they thought they could save money.

When I asked the winning supplier why they had not proposed the resilient system, they responded with a worry about the cost. Because they did not understand the magnitude of the business case, they decided to keep costs down by pushing the reliability and maintenance organization to the limit. Incidentally, within a short period of the installation going live, the customer bought a second system. This also had poor profitability for the supplier, since the customer was able to claim, with some justification, an unsatisfactory solution to the problem in the first place.

Establish implementation priorities and controls

During this step in the buying process, the sensible customer puts in the basics of project management. It is crucial at this stage to see the project in its entirety and to plan the milestones which allow the business and technical managers to control the implementation. The key is to document every action and to ensure that all the milestones have ease of measurement. It is not enough to state "Test system for user acceptance." The salesperson must describe the tests in detail and agree the measures of user acceptance.

Figure 3.1 shows a simple series of implementation controls. It concerns a proposal to use a smart-card as a means of accessing a voice system. This gives the clients of a stockbroker instant information on the prices of stocks and shares. The customer can also request access to a dealer who can take and execute orders to buy or sell.

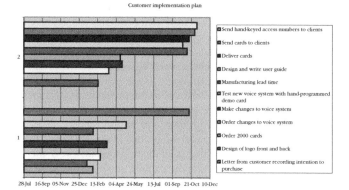

Fig. 3.1   Gantt chart of a customer implementation plan.

The job of a salesperson in this phase of the project plan is to suggest all the activities involved to ensure a successful implementation. Very frequently, there are issues of which the supplier is aware but which may be unknown to the customer. From previous experience, the supplier can anticipate some pitfalls and problems and avoid unnecessary surprises. It can be tempting to duck some of these issues and leave customers unaware of something they will probably have to face and solve in the fullness of time. Once again, competitive edge is available here. Someone else pointing out an additional factor unforeseen by the customer can damage the credibility of a competitor.

It is not possible to overstate the importance of getting this phase right and assisting the prospect to plan the project from the start, right through to successful completion. As we see in sales campaign planning (Chapters 6 and 7), no one buys anything until they fully understand what the outcome will be.

Select the exact functionality

This is the part of the project plan which the technical enthusiasts tend to enjoy. They survey the market for new technologies, study other implementations, and talk to lots of suppliers. From these ideas, and from a good knowledge of the future users of the new system, they produce the detailed functionality. Salespeople are also well aware of the work done at this stage. They have two concerns: using time wisely and meeting the customer specification.

First, is the customer using the salesperson's time wisely or is the customer wasting valuable selling time? When we deal with selling at different levels in campaign planning, we will need to look carefully at a problem in this area. We need to avoid the pitfall of two technicians, one the salesperson and the other the customer, spending lots of time looking at all the options now and in the future. It's all very well demonstrating all the possibilities, but if the customer has no commitment to doing something at all the appropriate levels, then the salesperson is better off devoting their time elsewhere.

It is easy for a salesperson to misunderstand where the customer is in the buying process. Customer technicians often start at "Select exact functionality" rather than "Set objectives" in order to identify the application and project goals. This can cost salespeople a lot of time.

The second point of concern for salespeople at this stage is to make sure that their products and services can do what the customer requires. From an understanding of their offerings and those of the competition, they will try to ensure that any unique elements in their portfolio have a place in the customer requirement.

The end of this stage in the process is the production of a document which outlines the exact specification of the technology the prospect wants to buy. It is a familiar document for experienced salespeople. The prospect writes a matrix of the shopping list down the left hand side, with boxes for all the competing supplier companies. The prospect then inserts a tick or a cross, depending on the presence or absence of a particular feature. It is crucial for salespeople to involve themselves in this phase. They will be at a significant disadvantage during the tendering process if their competition has the ear of the prospect and they do not.

Select the necessary products and services and their suppliers

Much of complex selling concerns this part of the process and the activities of the professional salesperson. However, it is necessary to first see what happens from a customer's point of view.

Senior management have a number of concerns. The key issue for them is that their managers choose the correct suppliers. This ensures that the project is successful, measured by "on time and within budget." They want the best deal possible, sometimes measured by "the cheapest," but in complex projects frequently described as "best value for money."

Another issue is that their managers subject the project to their normal tendering procedures. They want to be sure that no one places unreasonable pressure on their technicians or buyers such as would lead to them selecting a particular supplier and making a mistake.

Shareholders are very sensitive to any suggestion of sleaze or impropriety, and senior managers look carefully at procedures with this in mind. Some would say that all of this neutralizes the best salesperson. But, of course, when you buy the project you also buy the salesperson and the company they represent. Most people look for high standards of salesmanship and professionalism from companies with which they are about to do business.

The board looks at any capital investment project in terms of its relevance to the business and to its main strategies – "Is it hitting at the key issues we are facing and assisting with the implementation of our key strategies?" and "Is it part of our general direction and will it remain so for the life of the project?"

The board then worries about organizational change – "Does the project demand difficult or uncomfortable changes in organization?" or "Will the project still be relevant and feasible after we have made other planned changes?" This last issue is made more significant if the buyers and implementation managers of the project are unaware of the impending change.

The lower levels of management and staff involved in the buying process have different angles and motivations. All of these can have relevance to the buying company, and one of the great skills of salesmanship is to present the arguments to all the people involved in the way which suits their respective views.

Implement the project and train the users

During the implementation phase, the salesperson has the overriding concern of ensuring that the supplying company achieves its commitments. They will ensure that it meets all its deadlines and produces complete customer satisfaction by living up to expectations.

People often say, and it is certainly true, that the job of someone who sells complex solutions is as much about selling internally as to customers. When companies make complex proposals, particularly ones which involve new technologies, there is always a risk that something will go wrong. It is also frequently true that salespeople, during the sales campaign, have stretched the supplying company to make sure that the offering is competitive. This stretching process adds to the risk and it requires a dedicated salesperson to keep their company up to the mark.

There are, of course, good opportunities for the supplier in the training phase of the project. It is a chance to sell services and, if delivered professionally, the training courses will give good feelings to the delegates. The professional salesperson has a responsibility to present all the necessary training to the customer. They must try to ensure that neither the seller nor the buyer takes any shortcuts in what can be a crucial phase in a complex project. The lack of adequate training can be a major source of customer dissatisfaction.

Evaluate the results and adapt the project for improvement

The sensible customer will take this issue very seriously. In most cases, the technicians delivering a new system will liase with the users to find out whether it is producing what they require. They will also agree the necessary improvements. This iteration takes them back to the "Select functionality" phase of the project.

This type of evaluation is important, but the customer should not stop there. Equally important is to check that the project is producing the benefits agreed at the step which established the business case. There is a prevalent attitude which says: "We have spent the money and we are not going to go back to the old way, so why bother checking the return on investment?"

There are dangers in this attitude. If managers believe that no audit will take place, they will tend to produce business cases which are much more optimistic than they would otherwise be. Similarly, the skills in producing business cases will not develop unless managers monitor the results of each project.

A number of large companies have developed large, centralized systems. They have then made their user community adopt them as generalized systems. Finally, they have tinkered with the functionality and have failed to take a long, cold look at the benefits and relevance of their centralized processes. This has led to inappropriate systems and user dissatisfaction, sometimes on a very big scale. Sorting out the resulting situation is very costly, but if not undertaken will almost certainly cost the company the loss of competitive edge.

A further reason why a salesperson wants to assist the customer to audit cost justification is the need for reference sites. These are much more convincing if they can demonstrate business benefits as well as technical achievement. This checking mechanism takes the customer back to the business case. The other check is, of course, on the strategic relevance of the project. The customer needs to ask the question: "Is this still relevant?" or "Could we make changes to improve the project's contribution to the overall direction of the business?"

KEY LEARNING POINTS

» If the account manager is to be truly customer-facing, they will be with the customer as they undertake each stage in the process. It can be the definition of the difference between being a solution seller or just a seller.

» A seller will become involved with the project only when invited by the prospect at the "Select functionality" step or, even worse, at the step of "Select the necessary products and services and the suppliers of them."

» The solution seller, however, will involve himself from start to finish and may even instigate the whole idea by being the first person to identify the opportunity.

NOTE

1 David Clutterbuck & Stuart Crainer (1990) *Makers of Management*, Macmillan.

The E-Dimension
of Complex Sales

This chapter looks at the considerable opportunities that the e-dimension offers to sales managers and salespeople in terms of control and sharing of ideas.

Here are some facts surrounding the real situation in many organizations in developing complex sales campaigns.

» Sales managers often get sight of a complex sales proposal just before or just after submission to the customer. This means that it is too late for them to add value to the document even if they have information gained from other campaigns that would have improved the proposal considerably.
» Salespeople learn remarkably little from each other in terms of expressing vital parts of a sales proposal, such as the customer's basis of decision or the selling company's winning strategy. They may copy huge chunks of product description from marketing brochures, but are on their own when it comes to the vital part of a sales proposal – the executive summary.
» Many sales proposals are completed at two o'clock in the morning when there are no other salespeople to consult.
» The executive summary is often left until the last thing. This means that the focus of the sales campaign is not available to the selling team while they are dealing with the customer.

The e-dimension in complex sales solves all of these problems by using a simple electronic tool – the executive summary data sheet.

Imagine if each salesperson used this template to summarize the position in each complex sales campaign and everyone who needed it had access to it on the company's intranet. Salespeople, even at two o'clock in the morning, would be able to look at a number of previous executive summaries to look for the *mot juste* to describe a particular benefit, or a neat piece of purple prose that a salesperson had used in previous proposals to describe why an organization should buy from this particular company.

Think of the control the sales managers would have if they were able to go online and look at the current state of every sales campaign, or perhaps every sales campaign with a value greater than $50,000. Figure 4.1 shows what such an electronic tool looks like.

There is a completed example at the end of this chapter. The elements of the tool, and how to fill it in, are examined below.

THE **W.I.S.E.** TOOL

Title				
Name		Folder		
Team		Date		Status

		SCOPE OF PROPOSAL	WINNING STRATEGY	VALUES	
				One-off costs	
				Annual costs	
				One-off benefits	
BACKGROUND				Annual benefits	
		CUSTOMER NAMES	ACTIVITY	AGREEMENT	S
	C1				
	C2				
	C3				

		OPPORTUNITY OR PROBLEM STATEMENT	I	U
OPPORTUNITY/PROBLEM	O1			
	O2			
	O3			
	O4			

			SELECTION CRITERIA	CUSTOMER 'IDEAL'	S
BASIS OF DECISION	FINANCIAL	1			
		2			
		3			
	PRODUCT/SERVICE	1			
		2			
		3			
	PRACTICAL	1			
		2			
		3			

Fig. 4.1 WISEtool.

		PROPOSAL ELEMENTS		ONE-OFF	ANNUAL
PROPOSAL	Product	TVTdesserT range			
	Service	Rapid reaction delivery service			
	After sales service	Re-promotion for selected stores			
			TOTAL COSTS		

			BUSINESS BENEFIT		ONE-OFF	ANNUAL
BENEFITS	**TANGIBLE**	Increased revenues				
		Reduced costs				
		Avoid costs				
			TOTAL BENEFITS			
	INTANGIBLE	Management control				
		Customer satisfaction				
		Competitive edge				

		TASKS	START	END	Q1	Q2	Q3	Q4	Q5	Q6	Q7	Q8
IMPLEMENTATION PLAN	T1											
	T2											
	T3											
	T4											
	T5											
	T6											
	T7											
	T8											
	T9											
	T10											

		RECOMMENDED ACTIONS	OWNER	DATE
NEXT STEPS	A1			
	A2			
	A3			

Fig. 4.1 (*continued*)

EXECUTIVE SUMMARY DATA SHEET

Begin to prepare the data sheet the moment you have identified a sales campaign and agreed to carry it out. The earlier in the campaign you can answer the questions it raises, the clearer will be your strategy. This gives you selling focus and allows you to brief all the managers, product experts, and commercial people involved in the campaign so that they act consistently and support your overall approach.

It is unlikely for any campaign that you will have a full and satisfactory answer to every question, but the nearer you can get to that, the more likely you are to win the campaign, and, equally importantly, the easier it will be to produce an interesting and compelling executive summary for your senior customer managers.

This is an internal document but it contains everything you need to produce the executive summary for delivery to senior customer managers towards the end of the campaign.

Background

This makes the customer trust you as a salesperson or account manager, in terms of your having done the appropriate work and spoken to the appropriate people. You must also mention some of their people whom they trust. They are also immediately aware of what you are recommending. Perhaps more than anything, it demonstrates that your organization understands a lot about the customer's business.

» **Scope.** This explains the boundaries of your proposal. As succinctly as possible, it states what the opportunity or problem is that your customer is facing. It also shows how this proposal addresses the problem or opportunity and suggests the main benefit areas.
» **Winning strategy.** This is a short statement of why your organization will win this particular piece of business. After discussion with your team you should be able to identify the unique feature that differentiates your proposition. Once you have got this, it is a useful tool for communicating the strategy to anyone involved in the campaign. Do not be surprised if this strategy changes during the campaign.
» **Costs and benefits.** You will, of course, be able to enter the capital and revenue costs of your proposal simply as two figures. The

challenge is to be able to total the benefits that you have agreed with the customer. This depends on how close you have got to the people making the customer's business case. They are probably not the same people who will do any product evaluation. Your knowledge of the business case is a good demonstration of a supplier behaving like a collaborative partner rather than merely a supplier of commodities. Many large organizations have stated that they wish to create this type of relationship with their strategic suppliers.

» **Customer name, activity, and agreement.** Here you state the names of the customer's people you have worked with in preparing the proposal. In the actual summary document it will appear as something like: "We would like to thank Tony Phipps for his work in attending demonstrations and agreeing the technical viability of our proposal. Anna Howard gave us a lot of assistance in preparing the outline of the business case, and Ian Goddard gave us vital input to the implementation plan. Our thanks to all of them."

Under the headings on the data sheet, put down the key people you worked with, what you did with them, and what they have agreed that helps your case to move forward. The status box should be marked red, amber, or green, to show how far you have got during the campaign to get these important agreements.

The customer problem or opportunity

After reading this, managers will understand in more detail what the proposal is for and will have a snapshot of the business benefit that will occur. When we are selling to a customer, we are either solving a problem or allowing them to exploit an opportunity. State that here, with a reference to a person or a document to support the impact and urgency of the need.

» **Problem or opportunity statement.** Explain in the customer's terms what problem you are solving with this proposal or what opportunity you are helping them to exploit.
» **Impact.** In the summary you will comment on what you have been told of the impact of the problem or the significance of the opportunity. If necessary, you will mention the names of the people who gave you this information.

» **Urgency.** This records how urgent it is that the problem is solved or how significant it is from a competitive point of view for your customer to exploit the opportunity.

» **Value.** For each statement, give an indication of the value of the opportunity or perhaps the cost of the problem.

The basis of the decision

Now that the customer knows the problem or opportunity, we need to show them that we can see the decision to go ahead from the customer's point of view. In effect, we are telling them what to look for in our submission.

This section shows that you understand the issues which will affect the customer's decision to go ahead. It is normally useful to divide it into three subsections: *financial* – a statement of the customer's criteria for investment, if appropriate; *product* – a statement in customer terms of any product or technical considerations; and *practical* – a statement of the practical implementation issues, which shows that you are aware of them.

» **Selection criteria.** This is a statement of each decision criterion. During the sales campaign, try to discuss these with the appropriate people.

» **Feature of the "ideal."** Put down here what you have found to be the customer's ideal under each criterion. We may not be able to match it exactly, but this ideal will shape how we write the criterion in the executive summary itself. It is also useful, when using this document internally, to show where our proposal is hitting or missing exactly what the customer wants. The winning strategy must feature here, although perhaps in different words as you are looking at it from the customer's point of view. Prove that the customer needs the unique feature that you can supply.

» **Status.** Again red, amber, or green to show how much work we need to do to get nearer to the ideal.

The supplier proposal

This is a simple statement, in customer terms, of what we are proposing they buy and do. Try to avoid jargon. After the customer has read this, they will know what you are proposing.

» **Proposal elements.** Keep it simple and high-level. This is not the section that describes each feature and part number of your solution. Think of it from a senior manager's point of view – what does he or she *need* to know?
» **Capital.** The capital costs of each element.
» **Revenue.** The revenue or ongoing costs, probably on an annual basis.

Benefits

This gives the customer a clear idea of the business benefits and of who, in their organization, will take responsibility for achieving them.

» **Business benefit.** A statement of the customer's business benefit. To get to this, it is often useful to keep asking the "so what?" question. Write down the benefit. If it is difficult to see the connection between the benefit and a monetary reward to your customer, whether or not we can quantify that, ask "so what?" Eventually, you will get to a simple statement of the real benefit. Try to use the sub-headings to avoid mixing up solid financial benefits, such as a reduction in an existing cost, from less tangible (and therefore less compelling) benefits, such as an improvement in management control. Add in your unique benefit under whichever heading it fits.

Implementation plan

You and the customer, either separately or together, will probably have a project plan by the time it comes to writing the executive summary. Boil it down to (at most) 10 actions or groups of actions. Remember that the purpose of this section is to give senior management the confidence that the people concerned have thought the project through well enough to ensure that there is a high chance that the implementation will be successful. In the actual document, you will convert this into a Gantt chart.

Recommended actions

The objective of the executive summary is to encourage and persuade someone to do something. This section records what those short-term actions are. In most cases, you will include the recommendation that

THE W.I.S.E. TOOL

Title	Newstores TVTT
Name	Ken Leadbetter
Team	Newstores account

Folder	Newstores
Date	dd/mm/yy

Status	Amber

BACKGROUND

SCOPE OF PROPOSAL	WINNING STRATEGY	VALUES	
To sell the TVTdesserT range throughout Newstores, giving us sales revenues of £50,000 in the first year, and Newstores increased return from the Cabinet space required	We will demonstrate through a pilot scheme our rapid delivery service, and from customer satisfaction feedback the quality of the product	One-off costs	
		Annual costs	£56,000
		One-off benefits	
		Annual benefits	£25,000

	CUSTOMER NAMES	ACTIVITY	AGREEMENT	S
C1	K. Joseph	The head buyer, chilled foods, has looked at the promotion material and the product	He has agreed that a pilot should at leas pay for itself, and is looking for th e funds for their part in the promotion	A
C2	J. Biffen	Store manager, Leeds region	He has agreed to accept becoming a pilot store	G
C3	G. Howe	Financial controller, stores, is looking at the pilot figures	She will not agree unless the business case on quite low sales breaks even in the pilot	R

OPPORTUNITY/PROBLEM

	OPPORTUNITY OR PROBLEM STATEMENT	I	U
O1	In their strategy of increasing the sales of higher margin ready made meals, Newstores needs a luxury dessert range.	5	4
O2	The lack of a one stop store offering ready made meals to serve to guests could lead to lowering of competitiveness and fewer people through the door	7	7
O3	If the new range sells, there is an opportunity to increase, and easily measure the increase of margin made by the chill cabinets	4	6
O4			

BASIS OF DECISION

		SELECTION CRITERIA	CUSTOMER 'IDEAL'	S
FINANCIAL	1	Maximize the margin from cabinet space	Double the current product margin	A
	2	Minimize cost of pilot scheme	Should break even	A
	3	Minimize promotion cost of pilot	Supplier pays all promotion costs	A
PRODUCT/SERVICE	1	Maximum level of customer acceptance	60% of focus group agreed it is a good luxury product they would serve to friends	G
	2	Size and shape most suitable for chill cabinet space	No empty space	A
	3			
PRACTICAL	1	Maximize benefit from nationwide promotion	Promotion peaks at Christmas	G
	2	Maximize publicity locally for whole store offerings	Adverts promote other goods	R
	3	Maximize acceptance of the chosen pilot stores	All store managers signal their agreement	G

Complex sales figures.xls Page 1 of 2

Fig. 4.2 Completed WISEtool.

		PROPOSAL ELEMENTS		ONE-OFF	ANNUAL
PROPOSAL	Product	TVTdesserT range			£50,000
	Service	Rapid reaction delivery service			£1,000
	After sales service	Re-promotion for selected stores			£5,000
			TOTAL COSTS		**£56,000**

			BUSINESS BENEFIT		ONE-OFF	ANNUAL
BENEFITS	**TANGIBLE**	Increased revenues	Margin doubled on £100,000 of sales			£25,000
		Reduced costs				
		Avoid costs				
			TOTAL BENEFITS			**£25,000**
	INTANGIBLE	Management control				
		Customer satisfaction	High repurchase of the various products in the range			
		Competitive edge	One stop store for luxury dinner party ready made foods			

		TASKS	START	END	Q1	Q2	Q3	Q4	Q5	Q6	Q7	Q8
IMPLEMENTATION PLAN	T1	Place order for pilot stores	4-Apr-01	4-Apr-01		se						
	T2	Local promotion in pilot areas	1-May-01	31-Jul-01		s	e					
	T3	First deliveries	27-Apr-01			s						
	T4	Measure effectiveness of pilot scheme	15-Jul-01	20-Jul-01			se					
	T5	Nationwide promotion	1-Aug-01	31-Dec-01			s	e				
	T6	Rollout to all stores	21-Jul-01				s					
	T7											
	T8											
	T9											
	T10											

		RECOMMENDED ACTIONS	OWNER	DATE
NEXT STEPS	A1	Place order for pilot sites	K.J	dd/mm/yy
	A2	Presentation to pilot store managers	K.L	dd/mm/yy
	A3			

Fig. 4.2 *(continued)*

the customer should place an order for some or all of the elements mentioned.

Try it out. Think of an idea you want to get across to somebody at work or at play, and mull over the template. If what you are trying to persuade them to do is simple, then you might find that you hardly need more than 100 words to fill in the summary, but if it is more complex you might find that it becomes two pages or the equivalent in conversation. Try it with kids. If you keep it interesting enough to make them listen, you will certainly overcome their logical resistance to going to bed. If they remain obdurate despite your organized diplomacy, take their favorite gun off them and replace the recommended action plan part of the template with the parental stopper, "Because I said so."

Figure 4.2 shows the completed WISEtool.

CONCLUSION

This electronic tool, and the platform that gives access to it, is available through SofTools Ltd at: www.SofTools.net

KEY LEARNING POINT

One of the greatest problems facing sales managers is to get salespeople to help each other by sharing experience. If they build an electronic process into the selling cycle and insist on its being carried out like any other business process, then they can solve this problem. The benefit to the salespeople is that they save time by using the work previously done by their colleagues in planning and documenting winning propositions.

The Global Dimension of Complex Sales

This chapter looks at the threat posed by global stakeholders in complex sales planning in terms of:

» making sure the selling team have identified all the worldwide stakeholders; and
» involving stakeholders worldwide at the appropriate time in the customer's buying process.

To some extent, it could be said that the global dimension of complex selling offers opportunities. The global dimension means that any sale made to a large multinational in one geographical area can, in theory at least, be replicated in many other areas. But while this may be good for your organization, generally speaking it is not of any great benefit to the original seller in the primary location. If that is the case in your organization, then I am afraid that the global dimension opens up a number of threats to a complex sales campaign.

The problem is the danger posed by someone, somewhere in the world, getting involved at a late stage in a sales campaign and putting a block on what the selling team is proposing to local managers. It happens often. A selling team has put resources and money into a complex campaign in the UK, say, only to discover that the head office in the US does not have the "rubber-stamping role" that local managers had promised the salespeople, but carries out a real evaluation of the proposal with the added threat that something like the selling team's project is already happening in the US. Local buyers thus become locked into a battle to get their own way, and at best the sale is delayed while the issue is debated across the Atlantic, or at worst the proposal is blocked and an alternative solution implemented in deference to head office.

The trick is to identify all the people as early in the selling process as possible, persuading your local contacts to come clean about who else in the world will have an interest in what you are about to propose. Some of these people may not translate into "key people," but they need to be identified nonetheless and, in police terms, "eliminated from your enquiries." So, the key people we will talk about in the complex sales process are those with a direct role to play in evaluating proposals and making the decision, but early on in the campaign we will go through another analysis process – stakeholder analysis – which identifies the worldwide interest in the complex campaign.

Calling this process "stakeholder analysis" has two other aspects. The first is that there may be, on a global basis, a number of interested people in the selling company as well as in the buying organization. There may be project managers in Japan who are working on the next development in the products you intend to propose, or financial managers in the European head office who are working on different finance deals that will significantly alter the costs to your customer of ownership, or whatever. Remembering the salesperson's gloomy mantra – "If something can go wrong in a sales campaign, it probably will" – always check through the overseas side of your own organization when producing a complex plan.

The second aspect is that if there is no global dimension involved on either side, you can miss out this part of the process, relying on the identification of key people to reveal with whom you will have to deal during the campaign, and what you will have to do with them (see Chapter 7).

IDENTIFYING STAKEHOLDERS

A stakeholder in a complex sale is any individual or group of individuals who is/are affected in any way by the sale. They may be subcontractors, people who will have to supply different products and services, or members of the buying company's global purchasing department. There may certainly be a lot of them – if a number of your customer's people are *not* going to be affected by the campaign you are about to carry out, then why are you doing it at all, and how have you stated the campaign goal?

The stakeholders will include your customer's bosses, locally and in other parts of the world. Think about other teams. Is your proposal going to be unsuccessful if other teams in the buying organization do not agree with it or do not buy into the implementation? This may be very positive. If, for example, you are selling a different system for logging calls to the manager of a help-desk in the UK, would there be extra benefits to your customer if the system were adopted Europe-wide? If the answer to this is yes, then it is much more sensible to get their buy-in before you start your campaign, rather than trying to persuade them to go the same way after the event.

Now think about other people who could be working in the same area. In the end, everyone becomes aware of the new methods and processes available to them to improve their performance. It is very unfortunate if customer managers keep important projects to themselves so that they can earn Brownie points by being the first to make a change. How much better it would be if instead they looked for the

Table 5.1 Stakeholder analysis.

Stakeholder	I/E	Interest or involvement	I	+/−	S

Brownie points attracted by the manager who leads a collection of peer-groups towards some improvement in the way they do things.

Consider whether anyone has implemented a similar project in the fairly recent past. If so, then they should certainly be on your stakeholder list. Their input could be invaluable in helping you make the sale or avoid being blindsided at a later stage.

So, how do you pull all this together and document it? Take a look at Table 5.1.

The stakeholder column identifies the individuals or groups that will be most involved or impacted by this proposal. The next column says whether they are internal or external to the organization of the salesperson. It is worth noting that stakeholders abroad can be much more difficult to control, and may therefore need a higher level of monitoring. Now write down why the individual or group is involved in the project and what the impact will be on them or what their involvement will be.

The column marked "I" allows you to answer, on a scale of 1–5, the impact the stakeholder may have on the decision. If they could make or break the sale you will score them 5; if their impact, for or against, is minimal, then score them 1. When you are running the campaign, you will of course pay more attention to the stakeholders who score highly here.

Next, document their current attitude to the decision on a scale of +5 to −5. A score of 5 means that the stakeholder is strongly supportive of your case; zero means that they are neutral; and −5 means that they believe the proposal is ill-conceived and will try to stop its implementation. The column marked "S" is the status column and is marked red, amber, or green, depending on the amount of work that you are going to have to put in with each particular stakeholder. If there is little to do, mark it green; if the stakeholder could pose a big problem, mark it red.

These numbers will change as you go through the complex sales planning process and as you communicate with the stakeholders to try to get their enthusiastic support.

Table 5.2 shows a worked example of a stakeholder analysis in the case of making a fairly small software sale, designed to change how the customer's salespeople tender for business in a technology company by writing more customer-oriented executive summaries.

And that's just for quite a simple proposal!

INVOLVING GLOBAL STAKEHOLDERS

This is an interesting area of complex selling that frequently goes wrong. The only certainty about any complex project is that the jobs of some people around the world are going to change. Most large organizations are getting better at managing such change. There are, however, still some, along with many smaller businesses, who handle this part of the process at best insufficiently and at worst insensitively. This imperils the implementation of the decision, and is further complicated if the implementation is worldwide.

Incidentally, do not confuse involving stakeholders with training. It is helping the people involved to understand the benefits of the changes that the decision involves to their company, their customers, and themselves.

UPSETTING KEY PEOPLE WITH TECHNOLOGY

A good illustration of this point is a case in which I have been involved. It concerns the handling of a major Electronic Point of Sale (EPOS) upgrade decision by a large multinational supermarket chain. The chain in question had some 200 sites in the UK and Europe and intended to introduce advanced EPOS, first at a pilot site and then throughout the group. The following objectives were set:

» to reduce time at the checkout and improve customer satisfaction;
» to improve stock control and shelf-stocking activity;
» to improve the productivity of checkout operators; and
» to improve job satisfaction, in both the front-of-store and back-of-store areas.

Table 5.2 Stakeholder analysis – worked example.

	Stakeholder	I/E	Interest or involvement	I	+/−	S
A	Customer marketing	E	Started the process off; is looking for a template to write summaries faster	4	0	A
B	Customer salespeople	E	Will have to be motivated to implement the decision	5	−1	R
C	Existing user of your system in the USA	E	Salesman who could turn out to be a champion of the decision	5	4	G
D	Customer IT group – home country	E	Will have to instal the software	5	0	A
E	Customer IT group – USA	E	Will have to "rubber-stamp" proposal	1	0	A
F	Financial controller – home country	E	Might have to OK the financial case	3	0	A
G	Financial controller – USA	E	Trying to freeze expenditure because the US business is doing badly; they do not take into account how well the subsidiaries abroad are doing	5	−5	R
H	Customer sales directors – worldwide	E	Would be needed if the project is to go worldwide	3	0	A
I	European marketing manager	E	Could put a spanner in the works if they have a different idea	2	0	G
J	Production	I	May have to modify the tool to meet the precise need; must come up with a feasible cost	4	5	G

Given the volumes, margins, and stock sensitivities of a supermarket, all the objectives were easy to build into a business case. Senior management recognized that the project would add many millions of pounds to the bottom line.

The IT people chose hardware and software and carried out training – in the case of the UK pilot site, well before the implementation. Engineers installed the equipment at the pilot site. Because it passed its acceptance tests, and management looked forward to the results, all the stakeholders had been involved throughout.

The first pilot abroad, however, was a disaster. Every single objective area produced a negative result. The checkout queues were longer and shelf-stocking actually got worse. Customers' frustration led them to action that is the store manager's nightmare – they abandoned full trolleys near the checkouts. The process of replacing these items on the shelves was almost as expensive as throwing away the whole lot. Staff were so upset that key and long-serving people were leaving or threatening to do so.

What had gone wrong? The ensuing post mortem drew the conclusion that it was the early stage of the project that had misfired. The people in the overseas stores were unaware of what was happening until equipment started to arrive.

The implementation managers found a simple solution for the roll-out to other countries. During the build-up to each supermarket installing the advanced EPOS, local management arranged a series of activities guided by a package of material developed centrally.

Thus, store managers received a box of materials. Instructions helped them to put up posters at appropriate times, signalling the approach of the new technology. Store managers distributed newspapers with information on advanced EPOS, including crosswords and competitions to add some interest.

By the time training was due, staff were comfortable with the concept and the implementation proceeded smoothly. In the event, the number of people involved with giving training courses abroad diminished and the simple process of involving staff at an early stage paid for itself time and time again.

So, the global dimension presents a threat to the complex sales planner, one which is best met by grasping the nettle and tackling all the stakeholders here and abroad. It can be hard work, but it is work that is repaid handsomely, even if you only prevent one campaign a year from being wrong-footed by the sudden emergence of another key person in the decision, and/or one implementation failing disastrously.

KEY LEARNING POINTS

» The global dimension in a complex sales campaign poses threats as well as opportunities to the salesperson.
» To avoid the threat it is vital to do a thorough job in identifying all the stakeholders in any campaign – worldwide. The salespeople may not have to deal with all of them, but if they know who they are they can use their normal contacts to check that someone overseas will not become a blocker later in the campaign.
» The global dimension also gives the salespeople opportunities in terms of spreading a working solution from one part of an organization to others worldwide.

The State of the Art – Winning Complex Sales Campaigns

This chapter looks at the elements involved in creating a team-built sales campaign plan:

» the objectives and organization of a complex sales plan; and
» the definition of a good objective by the acronym "SMART".

OBJECTIVES AND ORGANIZATION OF A CAMPAIGN PLAN

First, here are the objectives of planning for complex sales:

» to agree the starting point from the prospect's point of view;
» to agree the starting situation of the selling organization;
» to agree the overall objective(s) of the campaign;
» to set milestones on the way to the objective in order to be able to monitor the implementation of the plan;
» to identify the resources required to implement the plan and win the business;
» to produce a detailed list of actions required to win the business;
» to identify skills deficiencies in the sales team; and
» to get the team's and management's complete buy-in to the action plans and resource plan.

The process described below is relevant for any sales campaign which can be said to be complex, that is one where there are a number of people involved in the buying process and a team involved in the selling. Having decided that, on the face of it, the campaign is about business that we want and which we can win, we can start to organize the process.

Getting the timing right

It is of little value to call the team together too early, before the customer has reached, either with you or without you, that part of the buying cycle which identifies the objective of some putative investment. However, you can be too late as well. To pull the team together just as the customer is about to make a decision also leads to a less productive planning session.

There is, frankly, little that can be done to influence the way the campaign is going, and the team will simply produce a situation report which will record the fact that they are likely to win or likely to lose. The best test for the right time to get into the process is whether or not the selling team can produce a meaningful campaign goal. The team needs to be able to state what they are going to try to sell and what overall benefit the customer is going to gain.

Experience shows that the right time to do the original plan is when the customer is at least some way through the buying cycle, but still some significant time away from the decision on suppliers (see Chapter 3). If we take a lengthy buying-cycle, then we should probably consider the time right when the customer is at least three months from a decision date but not more than nine months away. These matters are complicated by customers frequently being unable to set, and stick to, a decision date, but common sense should tell us when we need to get the team together.

Setting the campaign goal

Getting this first step right is a vital part of the planning process. It enables the team to focus their efforts on an agreed aim and allows them to check with the customer that they are reading the situation correctly. As with all objective-setting which we will deal with in this book, a campaign goal must obey the following rules. To be an acceptable statement of the team's aim, a goal must be "SMART":

» **S**tretching;
» **M**easurable;
» **A**chievable;
» **R**elated to the customer; and
» **T**ime-targeted.

Each element is examined below in more detail and in the context of a hypothetical example.

» **Stretching.** There is no point in wasting precious selling time on planning a sale which is going to occur even if the selling team took time out to go on a cycling tour of the Scottish Highlands – the job has to be difficult enough to merit the time required to set the plan.

Further, it is the role of the sales person to change the world. They need to set goals which test the team's ability to be persuasive – i.e., to change the mind of the customer so that they will do something different or larger. Often, a good campaign-planning session will change or add to the goal as the team examine what the opportunities are. If this happens, it is indeed right to change the goal. With all elements of the plan, you need to remain flexible to an ever-changing environment and new ideas. The overall goal is no exception to this rule.

» **Measurable.** The normal measure of a campaign goal is a sum of money which the team is going to achieve in sales revenues or in profits. In theory, the team should be interested in both and set a target which predicts the order value and the resultant profit. In practice though, many companies, for good reasons, do not give the profit responsibility to the team and the team may not be able to predict profitability.

In most cases it is unlikely that the selling company can be very accurate with this number at this stage. The team needs, however, to make an estimate to ensure that the plan is worth doing and that they can get a rough grip of what products and services will be required to solve the customer problem.

» **Achievable.** Having made certain that the goal is stretching, the team must also believe that it can be achieved. Normally, a customer is planning capital investment all the time, and the selling team should be sufficiently close to the customer to recognize where there is a feasible chance of success.

The achievable test is particularly important where totally new technology is envisaged, which the customer will recognize as carrying extra risk. Salespeople often fall into the trap of seeing an opportunity and proving a good business case, but then losing because not enough people within the customer's organization were willing to propose the risk to senior management. The key to checking achievability is to ask the question of as many people as possible inside the customer's organization and at as high a level as possible.

» **Related to the customer.** Just as we must be able to see what is the benefit of the campaign for the selling company in terms of revenues and profits, we must also get a flavor of what is in it for the customer. In the action of checking the campaign goal with the customer, the wording of this can be useful in terms of getting the customer's agreement on the main benefit statement which the salesperson will use in the sales campaign.

» **Time-targeted.** The date of completion of the goal completes the rules of setting appropriate objectives. It is uncanny how many sales campaigns are targeted to end by the date of the completion of the selling company's financial year! Once again, the concentration must be on the customer's view – is the timescale suitable for them as well for the selling company?

Example of SMART

A company is going to run a major sales campaign to sell products and services to a major electricity company that wishes to implement a new call-center.

» **Stretching** – the goal starts off stretching enough, as the company wishes to sell $1,350,000 of hardware and $1,500,000 of systems consultancy, design, and implementation.

» **Measurable** – the objective is already measurable, although in this case the sales team can only measure (or estimate) the campaign goal in broad terms, i.e., to sell $1,350,000 of hardware and $1,500,000 of systems consultancy, design, and implementation.

» **Achievable** – the proposed solutions involve extension and amendment to systems which are already in place, so there is little technology risk. However, there are dangers involved in the enormous change which the organization and its people will have to accept and implement. It will be stretching to help the customer face those risks, but on balance the objective looks achievable.

» **Related to the customer** – as well as the benefits to the selling company (i.e., the sale of $1,350,000 of hardware and $1,500,000 of systems consultancy, design, and implementation), the benefit to the customer is that it receives a call-center which in time will become the single interface with its customers. This will improve customer service and reduce the number of calls customers have to make to achieve a satisfactory result. At the same time, the customer will reduce the costs and staffing levels of its current telephone response centers.

» **Time-targeted** – regardless of when the seller would like completion to occur, it must also fit in with the customer's expectations and needs. By the same token, it must be within a timescale that is acceptable to both sides, since there is the question of whether implementation can physically be done within the agreed timescale (which is also an aspect of achievability).

Now check the campaign goal with the customer

Some salespeople are uncomfortable with the prospect of showing the customer the basis for a sales campaign. They worry that the customer will balk at a price given too early, or a timescale with which they cannot agree at that stage.

However, the logic of this is hard to accept. In solution selling we are always trying to understand why the customer will *not* buy as well as why they will. The earlier we know about any objection in the mind of the customer, the better we can make our plan to deal with it. A simple trial close can give a good return and add to the plan significantly.

> **Seller:** "We are aiming to supply the solution for completion of the installation by the end of July."
>
> **Buyer:** "No way. There will be a bottleneck on the engineering effort required, which makes that date far too optimistic."
>
> **Seller:** "If we could show you an implementation plan which identifies those engineering resources and gets implementation completed by July, would you consider it?"

The vigor with which the customer sustains this objection will tell the seller how feasible is the earlier date. In any case, the discussion of the campaign goal has started the process well by identifying the concerns of the customer which, if not dealt with, will become objections to the sale.

THE CAMPAIGN PLANNING PROCESS

The step-by-step detail of this process in practice can be found in Chapter 7, but here some general principles are examined.

In a complex campaign, environmental analysis concerns the customer's buying cycle, the customer's reasons for buying, and the seller's qualification of the prospect. Qualifying the prospect deals with whether we can win the business and whether the profit available is worth the effort we will have to put in. Expressed as a diagram, it looks like the chart in Figure 6.1.

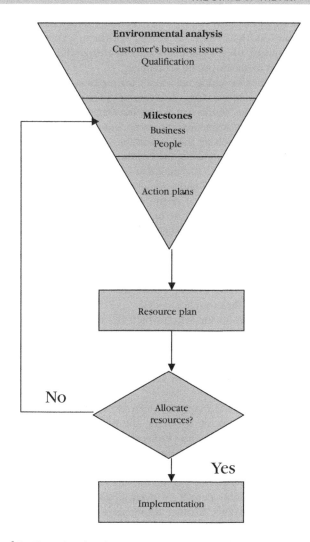

Fig. 6.1 Campaign planning process.

The shape of the chart is driven by experience which has identified that if it takes one unit of time, say an hour or a day, to set the milestones for the campaign, then it takes two units to analyze the environment and half a unit to decide on the action plan.

When it comes to setting milestones for progress in the sale, they are best divided into two types: the customer's business issues and the seller's people issues. In this way we are pursuing both the logic of the sale – i.e., what is in it for the customer – and also the psychological and people issues which are the focus of the skill of selling. Both areas are essential. If we do not assist the customer to prove their business case, someone else may do so, and if that someone else is a competitor then they will be gaining competitive advantage.

Besides, if there is no real financial and strategic reason for the customer to buy, someone in the organization is going to call a halt. This person is frequently quite high up in the customer organization and the damage done is more than just wasted selling effort – it is also the loss of reputation with an influential person. The customer's first impression of the selling company will be that they pursue sales for their own exclusive benefit, rather than checking that there is something in it for the customer as well.

Another problem for the seller, which is a result of the inevitable delay caused by a poor business case, is an internal one – the accounts manager probably twisted arms and struggled to ensure the availability of resources to carry out the next step, and the embarrassment caused by the delay will also turn into a loss of credibility the next time resources are sought.

Although a project is frequently delayed because of the lack of a good business case for the customer, the people issues are equally important. Once the selling team can see what they need to achieve to win the business, they can start the activity plans. The key to making the activity plans practical is accountability – each action must have an owner who has accepted the job and the timescale for it.

Remember that only people involved in the creation of the plan can be assigned actions. If other resources are required to make a contribution, then a member of the planning team is given the action to liaise with the managers of those resources and to get their agreement to the action and the timescale.

RESOURCE PLANNING AND THE MANAGEMENT REVIEW PROCESS

Any planning process ends up with a number of goals or milestones, together with a series of actions which the team are committed to take in order to achieve those goals. Resource planning should be a simple re-sort of the activities by resource.

The team know what results they are striving for and have established what they need to do. They are now in a position to inform management of the plan. They take their resource plan to the managers responsible for the required resources of people, machinery, and money. A decision is made.

This is a crucial time in the life of the plan. When the selling team makes its presentation, both sides – management and the team – must be clear whether the review is to look at the quality of the plan or whether it is to commit resources to the implementation.

Management will have lots of submissions to look at. If they are at the stage of the financial year where they are reviewing plans all around the organization before making decisions on resources, then they must make this absolutely clear to the team.

Let us assume that both management and the team are certain that a review meeting is going to make decisions on resources. Lots of things can still go wrong, particularly in an organization which is in the throes of putting formal planning into its selling teams.

The best way to approach the meeting is in terms of a contract. The selling team propose the result which they believe they can achieve, which, as has been seen, is normally measured by sales revenues and/or profit. They also produce the resource plan which they believe is required if the goal is to be achieved. It is management's prerogative to question, and suggest changes to, the action plans and consequently the resource plans.

They are in a position to suggest work which has already been done elsewhere and which could offer the selling team some shortcuts. Very significantly, they are in a position to know whether or not the resources requested have the necessary knowledge, skills, and experience to carry out the actions assigned to them. This, too, can change the plan or, in extreme cases, invalidate it.

In the end, the agreement is made and the contract accepted – "We will give this result if you will give us these resources." There is an important point still to be remembered by both sides – all contracts, particularly stretching contracts, are taken in good faith with "best intentions" on both sides. Sometimes one or other of the parties will fail. Just as the selling team can give no guarantee of success in a competitive world, so management will sometimes fail in their endeavors to provide the promised resource. It is entirely possible that, for example, a missed deadline on a product improvement occurs – the key is for both sides to recognize and acknowledge the risks.

The whole thing can go hopelessly wrong if the company culture becomes one that falls short of openness on the part of all or any of the parties involved. If the selling team get the impression that any proposal they make is going to be accepted by management as good, but that management will then require the team to achieve it with much less resources than are in the plan, then the selling team will add a little to the resource plan in the first place, knowing that it will be cut.

If management feel that any proposal which the selling team make will be less than can be achieved, and could take more resources than actually required, then a vicious circle starts. Worse still, opportunities will be lost where the selling team make an assumption that the resources will not be available to them.

In a mature planning organization, the results are stretching but achievable, the resources sensible, and the people expected to work professionally. In such a case, this initial review will produce an agreed contract which, with best efforts, will succeed. Further review will occur as time passes, the team make progress, and things change.

STEP-BY-STEP THROUGH THE CAMPAIGN PLANNING PROCESS

By now, the team have in mind a campaign goal and have agreed with an appropriate senior manager within the customer organization that it obeys the rule of being a "SMART" objective. The salespeople now need to assemble the team to validate the goal and produce the campaign plan. In common with all business decisions, there is always an element of the unknown. As you discover holes in your knowledge base, note them down in the plan. Then when you come to action-planning you can put one of the team members in charge of collecting the facts which are missing.

How long the team should allow

This is a difficult question to answer. If the team are new to the process and the campaign goal is big enough to merit it, you should allow two days. This is sufficient time to do a thorough job on the environmental analysis, decide as a team the milestones involved in achieving the goal, and agree an action plan. It is also enough time to prepare and carry out a management review, either to inform management of the plan or to obtain agreement to the resource plan.

Although, in theory, the team should continue with the process for as long as it takes for them to be satisfied with the quality of the work, in practice most teams need a time-target. The prior agreement of a manager to attend a briefing at, say, 3.45pm on the second day, gives a useful focus to the event. The team are aware that they need to have something sensible to say before that time. The timescale for an audit of an existing plan is shorter, say a day or even a more regular half-day.

Prior to the event

Here is a checklist of what needs to be done before the campaign planning is started in earnest.

» **Get the agreement of the team members and their management that they are committed to attend.** Try to do this well in advance and confirm the arrangement in writing. Planning tends to demonstrate its benefits some time after it has been done. You always run the risk, therefore, that a crisis which can be solved in the short term gets a higher priority on the actual day of the planning event. The planning team should include anyone who will be involved in the implementation of the plan, and should be accountable for some of the actions.

» **Agree a time for an appropriate manager to come and hear the plan review.** The most appropriate manager is the one who has the authority to agree all the resources. This person may not be available, because of the number of plans they would have to review, and a compromise may be necessary. It is certainly useful for the manager to have some control over some of the required resources.

» **Send out a briefing document to all team members.** Make sure that everyone is aware of the objectives of the planning event and of the putative campaign goal which the salesperson is going to propose. Set their expectations for what the event will have as its output. Emphasize that it is not only a think-tank but also a decision-making forum where they are going to be asked to commit themselves to actions and accountability for the completion of them.

Include in the briefing the minimum of information necessary for the team to be aware of the customer opportunity and to acquire a passing knowledge of your company's relevant products and services. The event itself is not the appropriate time to go into great detail, particularly on technical issues, so keep it short and simple.

» **Agree the customer input.** Campaign plans are normally created without reference to the customer. After all, you are going to get into detailed areas of politics and people, yours and theirs. It is a shame, however, to miss the opportunity to impress customers with the professionalism of the process you are going to use. They will probably be interested also in the fact that you and your company are taking the campaign seriously.

In this regard you may get further confirmation of how seriously the customer is approaching the matter. Few customer managers willfully allow a supplier to go to the sort of trouble and expense of running a planning session unless there is some intention on their part to do something about the problem or opportunity. It is often therefore a good idea to invite the customer to make a contribution to the plan, perhaps as an after-dinner speaker on the topic or during the event itself.

» **Choose a good location.** If it is possible, bring the technology with you to allow a member of the team, or someone brought in specially for the task, to produce the paper document at the end of the first day. This document is the hard copy of what the team has produced in flipchart form.

Assessing the customer's business issues

The first responsibility is to look at the customer requirement and ask searching questions about why, from a business point of view, the customer will buy.

» **What is the customer's business objective for this campaign?** In order to sell into the heart of a company and its direction, you need to understand how the project you are proposing fits into the company's strategy and direction. Use this question to try to compose a single sentence which connects the project with a major company strategy or vision.

Getting the customer's business objective right is important. It sets the theme of how we are going to interest and sell to every level of management in their organization. It is also a shortcut method of briefing anyone from the selling company on the overall reason why the customer is going to buy. If you have decided to involve the customer in your planning event, you may be able to agree this statement there and then.

» **What critical success factors (CSFs) declared by the customer does this campaign address?** Now broaden your search for how well the project fits the customer's strategy. You need to understand, from published material or from questioning the customer, what issues are believed to be critical to the customer achieving their business objectives. These are frequently identified in the company's annual report. Starting from there, you need to check again – at the highest level possible – whether the CSFs are still current. Such a conversation will also give you other ideas for fitting the project to the customer's strategy.

» **What benefits, both tangible and intangible, will the customer derive from a successful implementation?** This is a straightforward list of all the potential benefit areas. The list distinguishes tangible from intangible benefits. The difference is that tangible benefits can be reduced to a sum of money, whereas intangible benefits can be seen as useful but not quantifiable. Tangible benefits are much more persuasive to a board of directors than intangible.

» **What, roughly, are the amounts of expenditure involved?** Make a list of all the expenditure the customer will be involved in. This list needs to be comprehensive – make sure there are no hidden extras.

» **How does the *prima facie* return-on-investment case look?** Even at this stage, you and the customer can make a first draft of the cost-benefit analysis. The main holes in the case are likely to be in estimating the tangible benefits. In the action plan which will follow, you will put down activities such as meetings with line managers to gain their agreement to the quantification of the business case.

» **What key ratios will be the basis of how the customer measures the success of the project?** Directors and managers at all levels of a business have in their minds a number of key ratios. For example, first-line sales managers will be aware at most times what their sales revenues are to date compared to where they should be at this time of the company year.

Solution selling demands that we understand what financial ratios each of the key people holds important. From that knowledge we can tailor the presentation of benefits to illustrate the impact on those ratios which are personally important to those key people. We will not always be successful, as no project can be expected to hit the hot buttons of every executive involved, but it is a good challenge to try to be as comprehensive as possible.

» **Where, in terms of geography and company divisions, will the benefits occur?** If the product you are selling is going to have a wide impact, it is necessary to make a good list of where the benefits must be sold. At some point you need a groundswell of opinion moving towards a recommendation for your product – and the wider and louder this groundswell is, the better the chances of success.

» **What are the risks which the customer will take if they go ahead with this project?** This is not the detailed risk-analysis which a company looks at in calculating return on investment, but more a strategic look at the risks involved. Use the strategy statements from above – such as the customer's business objective for the project, or their CSFs – as a guide for this part of the exercise. Is this project, while consistent in theory with the customer's strategy and CSFs, putting any of these areas at risk?

» **How does the size of this project compare with others the customer has undertaken?** The reason for this question is that it forms the start of your process of qualifying the prospect. With the best will and best business case in the world, companies remain fearful of the unknown or the new. There is a big difference between examining the technical and financial case for putting in a huge new way of doing things, and taking the decision to do it. It is always easier to sell the second implementation than the first. Equally, it is always more likely that a customer will go ahead with a project if they have done something of a similar size before.

If this is a bigger, or geographically wider, venture than the customer has attempted before, the selling team need to take that into account in planning the campaign. Very deliberate actions will be put in place to try to build up confidence in the customer that the project implementation will be successful. Indeed, it may be very desirable to identify this risk in more detail – for example, it is not unusual to suggest that the customer buys some consultancy services to look at contingent risks brought on by a project.

KEY LEARNING POINT

The key to winning a competitive complex sales campaign lies in forming an agreed team plan, where the team agree on the way forward and managers of the resources necessary to implement the plan have agreed to release them at the required time. Implementing the plan in a controlled way can itself have a positive effect on the prospect, since they see the team reaching their milestones and carrying out actions in a predictable and professional way.

Complex Sales in Practice – Qualifying the Prospect

This chapter looks at the practical steps involved in creating a team-built sales campaign plan:

» qualifying the prospect;
» assessing the team's starting position; and
» a worked example.

There is a Chinese proverb which states: "Before you decide where you want to go and how you are going to get there, make sure you know exactly where you are now." In complex sales planning you have to add: "and make sure everyone involved agrees."

Some would regard the qualification of the prospect as the most important part of the planning process. The qualification process never stops. Professional salespeople are constantly assessing the changing position in the campaign. They are watching for signs – sometimes obvious, sometimes subtle – which tell them how they stand against the competition.

What follows is a consideration of a checklist which probes into the areas where salespeople need to ask hard questions and acknowledge the answers, even those which say that all is not going well. We will look at the process under the following headings.

» Customer need.
» Finance.
» Key people.
» Timescale.
» Solution.
» Basis of decision.
» Implementability.
» Competitive position.

We will also look at the subsidiary questions that arise under each heading, and the chapter ends with a worked example.

CUSTOMER NEED

In this part of the process the team examine what progress has been made on the completion of a customer business case on which the customer could make a decision to buy. The subsidiary questions are:

» is it a real need?
» is the requirement strategic to the customer? and
» is the campaign worth the necessary effort from the selling company?

Is it a real need?

The professional salesperson is well aware that all managers and technicians are interested in new things. The purchasing department of a large retailer will have people who are constantly monitoring the market, and the suppliers to it, for new products. Information and communications technology people at all levels are notorious for looking into new technologies, studying them until they understand them, and then dropping their interest as something which is two keystrokes better comes along.

Selling teams are on their guard for time-wasters and this question is a good starting point for establishing whether or not the prospect is seriously going to contemplate what you are proposing. The best test is to ask whether, if you were running your customer's business, you would buy this product and go into this new environment. If the answer is yes, then you have the start of a qualified prospect. If the customer at a high level also expresses a real need for the solution, then you have the beginnings of a runner.

The selling team may also have to prove that a competitive disadvantage will occur for those organizations that do not get into new technologies early. A stronger selling position would be to prove that a company will have a competitive edge from leading the field by investing now.

Is the requirement strategic to the customer?

The work that the team have done in assessing the customer's business situation will tell them the strength of their situation in this regard. If the team have already identified and sold the link between the project and the customer's strategy, then the team will score well here. If there are still a series of question marks, or if there are any mismatches, then the team will recognize that a lot of work needs to be done before they can give themselves a clean bill of health.

Is the campaign worth the necessary effort from the selling company?

This is the crunch. From the team's understanding of the customer's position and attitude to going forward with the project, they have to make a go or no-go decision. Not only that, but that decision must be revisited on a regular basis as the customer's stance develops and changes.

The customer need is not the only issue involved in the decision on whether or not to put in sales effort. All the subsequent points related to the selling company and its situation will be taken into account as well. But identifying a real need that is strategic for the customer to act on is the strongest basis for a campaign, and the absence of such a need is the weakest.

FINANCE

The subsidiary questions here are:

» is the money available in a budget?
» do all the people concerned have a rough cost expectation?
» has the necessary return-on-investment process been completed?

Is the money available in a budget?

Depending on the level of the account you are dealing with, you need to find out how budgets are set and whether some money has been, or could be, allocated to the project you are selling. Frequently, large companies have capital investment budgets separate from the day-to-day running budgets or revenue budgets. If possible, it is very desirable for a salesperson to know how these budgets are set and to what level they are delegated.

The delegation issue is important. Some boards will delegate portions of the capital investment budget to the next level of management, but insist that each major item of expenditure returns to them with a report and a recommendation on which they will then make a decision. Other boards will actually delegate the decision itself to the next level, or an even lower level. The trend now is towards more centralized control of capital expenditure budgets.

Having established where the budgets are, the selling team then have to establish whether any money has been allocated to the project or, failing that, whether there is a reasonable chance that the money can be found.

Do all the people concerned have a rough cost expectation?

In Chapter 6, the section on assessing the customer's business situation discussed the importance of letting everyone know what the cost of the project is likely to be. This subsidiary question records whether or not the selling team have grasped the nettle or ducked the issue.

Once again, level of seniority plays its part. It is not enough to find one manager who sees no problem in the money being found. Many salespeople have been blind-sided by a senior manager stepping in at the last moment or at any time in the campaign with the dreaded question " *How* much?", said in a tone of disbelief.

Has the necessary return-on-investment process been completed?

In the qualification process this question is a summary of the customer's attitude to RoI. Unusually, this is a case of a yes or no answer. Any organization big enough to require the attention of a sales team from a supplying organization will almost certainly have a business process for examining RoI. With or without a salesperson's knowledge, the buying company will put new projects through this process. There are rarely exceptions. The process is, of course, sometimes unnecessary if the sum of money required is trivial.

The team need to identify the key person on the buying side who is responsible for this and ask the direct question, "Has the project been evaluated, and did it pass?"

There is much debate about this among people involved in solution selling. Some people insist that it is too much like prying into the confidential business processes of the customer. A preferred school of thought, however, is that it is safer to be involved in this evaluation process than not to be involved and to take a risk. The risk is that activity is taking place inside the customer organization which could invalidate the sales campaign or some of the activities in the campaign plan. As usual, the customer holds the key. If you plan how to approach the customer with RoI in mind, be prepared with the arguments as to why you need to be involved in the internal process.

The fact is that the salesperson may very well be able to add value because of their knowledge of other companies who have been down the same route. A professional salesperson may be able to suggest costs which the buying team has not identified or, more importantly, assist the buying team to assess or quantify the benefits of the proposition.

Once the salesperson has made an attempt to argue their way into involvement in the process, the customer will deliver judgment, and that seems to be the safest course. When the arguments are not strong enough, or if there is a company policy which prohibits outsiders taking part in the financial exercise, the salesperson will get the brush-off, probably politely, but decisive nevertheless.

Under the topic of the basis of decision below, we will look at finding out what the RoI process is, but at this stage, the question of whether the necessary RoI process been completed is quite concrete.

KEY PEOPLE

The appropriate level of contact is probably the most difficult thing to get right in solution selling. In any buying decision there tend to be people who are doing the evaluation work and those who will agree that the evaluation should happen and decide on the outcome.

While the selling team are bound to spend a lot of time with the evaluators, it is vital that they retain regular contact with the other group of decision-makers. This can be a political minefield. Most salespeople have been told at some time or other that: "If you go above my head and sell to my boss I will make sure that you play no more part in this evaluation."

A variation on this is: "There is no point in your meeting the senior people – they will merely rubber-stamp my recommendation." In both of these cases, someone, often the technical buyers, is acting as gatekeeper and preventing the selling team having access to decision-makers. Once again, the salesperson needs to plan how they are going to prove the added value of having this access. You will not always succeed, but you have to try.

You need a statement from the top if you are going to understand the context of the proposed project. You need to hear the senior managers express their CSFs in order to aim your proposal at the heart of the business. It is important to use your senior management team well in this regard. Frequently, a request for the two managing directors to meet will have the necessary effect of facilitating access by the salesperson to a level otherwise denied.

In the qualification process the salesperson needs to answer the following subsidiary questions:

» do you know all the key people?
» do you have as good access to the key people as your competitors do?
» are the key people all informed of the pending buying decision?

Do you know all the key people?

In Chapter 5 we discussed identifying stakeholders worldwide who might have some involvement with the proposed project, in either the decision to go ahead or its implementation. The list of key people is much smaller and confines itself to those who are critical in the decision-making process. In discussion with your main contact, you should get fairly close to who is going to be involved. What you are looking for, though, is who the decision-maker is going to turn to for an authoritative opinion on some aspect of the project. The more people involved, the harder the campaign. The higher the individuals in the organization, the more difficult it will be to get regular contact with them.

The definition of this question is: "Can we, when we need it, get access to anyone involved in the process of evaluation on the customer's side?" It is not good enough to have had them in the corporate box at Lord's – it must be the potential to meet them in a timely manner in order to discuss the project (probably amongst other issues, too). If the project is big enough or important enough to the buying company, the list could include a lot of people. I have known campaigns where up to 50 people have had some involvement.

Do you have as good access to the key people as your competitors do?

Another litmus test. In some cases you will not succeed in getting contact with all the people involved – this second test then becomes crucial. You are on a very uneven playing field if the competition is talking to people to whom you do not have access. If these people happen to be the most senior managers in the buying organization, then this could be critical to your hopes of success.

Finding the answer to this question is also tricky. Your contacts may not know that the competition has high-level contact, or they could choose not to give you that information. Probe deeply and use your sales instincts as well as your questioning techniques. If you remember the golden rule of qualification – if any part of your campaign could be going wrong, then it probably is – you will pay enough attention to competitive level of contact to ensure that you are not fighting the bidding battle with a considerable handicap.

Are the key people all informed of the pending buying decision?

As with all these qualification questions, this one is another effort to ensure that the customer is as committed to action as you are. Having understood who will be involved in the decision-making process, the team now have to check that each and every one of the key people is aware that a buying decision is planned.

In many instances where a sales team has insisted on involving all the key people early on, a skeptic or someone likely to veto the decision has been discovered. Such a discovery does not necessarily mean that the campaign is over, but it does mean that the team, probably with the help of someone in the customer organization, need to make sure that such a person agrees to have an open mind. The other point about speaking to all the key people early on is that you will detect their opening attitude to the proposed investment.

TIMESCALE

Whereas the "key people" question is one of the most important, the "timescale" question is one of the most difficult to answer authoritatively. The human condition leads, in the main, to postponing decisions and avoiding change. A professional solution-seller is almost constantly proposing significant change and suggesting that a decision is made soon and urgently.

There is a conflict here, which comes to a head when you are trying to tie someone down to a decision date. There is no magic answer. If, in the end, a customer decides to postpone a decision or a project, that is their prerogative. All the salesperson can do is persistently probe for the feasibility of a decision and an implementation date.

In pursuing the timescale question, salespeople are also checking that the customer is actually in a position to buy. The credibility of a sales forecast depends on the degree to which the salesperson can convince their manager that the customer is realistically in a position to go ahead.

The two subsidiary questions here are:

» have the key people agreed on a decision date?
» is there an agreed implementation timescale?

Have the key people agreed on a decision date?

Funnily enough, this is more likely to be the case when a tender is in progress. If a customer goes out to a number of suppliers and requests a proposal or quotation, it is quite probable that at the same time they will give out a date for the proposals to be in and, at least by implication, a decision date.

It is more difficult to pin down a date during the early investigation phase. That is, before the customer has arrived at that stage in the buying process that we have called "select the necessary products and services and their suppliers" (see Chapter 3). It is also more difficult to get an agreed date where there is no competition involved – for example, when additional functionality is being added to an existing service.

A thorough understanding of the customer's business processes will help with getting a secure answer to this question. If you know, for example, when the customer needs to get a recommendation ready to go to a particular board meeting, then you will be in a position to predict to which meeting it could feasibly go. If you are involved in the customer's RoI process, then this will be a further clue as to when a decision could be made.

In the end, you ask the question of everyone you meet, and then ask them again when you meet them again. Listen hard to the manner in which the answer is given, as well as the answer itself, and you will detect the degree of certainty or reliability of the response.

One more thing on this topic – begin to ask the question early in the campaign; for example, at the first meeting. People are happier to take a commitment when the date of delivering it is a long way off. It is easier to get an agreed date in three months' time than to try to tie someone down to making a decision next week, so try to get the date agreed well in advance.

Is there an agreed implementation timescale?

However clever a product is and however much a customer needs it, the solution suggested by the product must be buyable and implementable. I have discovered great opportunities for competitive edge when I was the first salesperson to work with the customer to produce the outline of an implementation plan. Some people call this "timetable-selling." During the opening call with a prospect or customer on a particular campaign, a professional seller will try to get them to assist with the creation of a bar-chart which identifies all the major milestones in the implementation of the proposed project. Do not duck issues here. It is safer to talk about some difficult phase in the evaluation or implementation well in advance of the problem occurring. The modification of this forms part of all subsequent calls and, of course, the requirement for a decision date to be part of the implementation plan is clear.

SOLUTION

So far, the emphasis in the qualification process has been on the buyer's situation. We need now to turn to the seller's side. The proposed solution should have a number of attributes. First and foremost, it must solve the customer's problem or assist the customer to exploit an opportunity.

Next, it must represent good business for the selling company. The main measures for this are profitability and risk.

The third attribute is a "nice-to-have" rather than an essential. It is whether or not the project will lead to further business with the same customer and act as a reference to improve the chances of selling the solution to other prospects and customers.

The three subsidiary questions are:

» is your solution valid?
» is the risk of your being able to deliver your promises acceptable?
» is the project profitable, now or through future sales?

Is your solution valid?

It is unlikely in a complex project that any solution offered will meet every single detail of the customer's specification. Most decisions of this nature have some compromise built in. The key for the selling team is to ensure the validity of their offering.

It must be a solution to the problem *and* give the benefits described in the customer assessment and business case. It must also fit in with the strategic policies and direction of the customer, which again were identified in the customer assessment part of the planning process. Given a positive response to these issues, the only other test of validity varies according to each particular customer – will they agree that the way you are suggesting is a valid answer to the problem?

Is the risk of your being able to deliver your promises acceptable?

A salesperson may have to do a lot of internal selling to get a positive answer to this. Many organizations have a business process aimed at getting the agreement of all parties concerned – from the finance people to the engineers – that the risk is acceptable and fits into the selling company's strategy.

Is the project profitable, now or through future sales?

Once again, this is often put into a business process whereby the salesperson has to produce an estimated profit and loss account for the project. The level of profit required will obviously vary for each particular project. At the most profitable end will be repeats of previous sales of high-value products, while at the lower end will be loss-leaders, where the whole reason for the sale is concerned with other sales which will flow from them.

BASIS OF DECISION

Establishing the basis of decision is said by many to be the key technique which separates the solution seller from the product salesperson or box-shifter. It involves understanding, from the customer's point of view, all the issues surrounding the sale. It is useful to break down the basis of decision (BoD) into the following three areas:

» the financial basis;
» the technical basis; and
» the practical basis.

Financial basis of decision

In the section on finance above, at the start of the qualification process, we posed the question: "Has the necessary RoI process been completed?" The financial basis of decision is concerned with finding out what that process is. The salesperson has to find an authoritative answer to the question: "How does the customer, as an organization, carry out investment and RoI appraisal?"

Technical basis of decision

This part of the BoD tends to be the part on which most emphasis is placed. It is the statement by the company's technicians of the functionality that they require. It will go into great detail and be used as a template to compare the relative merits of each rival supplier's proposal.

Assuming that there are advantages and disadvantages for each proposal, the BoD will alter as different weightings are put on different functions. Indeed, every technical presentation and demonstration is aimed at altering the BoD by moving it towards the unique features of the supplier making the presentation.

It is this ebb and flow in the BoD which these questions chart, and it is vital to use them frequently to measure progress. Having said that, the technical BoD is by no means the only way that a customer will weigh up the merits of the bids on offer, but it is the one into which the selling team will put a lot of effort and which can sometimes blind the team to other issues which surround a complex decision.

Practical basis of decision

The third area which will dictate how a customer examines a project is its practicality. At this stage in the qualification process the team are trying to understand the ground rules – what is important to the customer in terms of the impact on their people. Is the customer looking for ease of use or is minimum disruption of current processes during the implementation the key issue? Will the change be accepted willingly by the people concerned? And so on.

A further possible BoD on practicality grounds is organizational change. You may find management laying down a rule that no project will be entered into if it requires further organizational change. This frequently occurs when the company has recently completed a big change for other reasons. Senior managers are aware that it is desirable to let an organization settle down from time to time.

The subsidiary questions on BoD are:

» have you agreed with the key people their criteria for deciding to go ahead?
» have you influenced this?

Have you agreed with the key people their criteria for deciding to go ahead?

Ask, and keep asking, so that by the time it comes to making your proposal you can put it in their terms, not only from the business case point of view, but for all the key issues which surround the buying decision and the implementation.

Have you influenced this?

The professional salesperson tries to get the customer to agree, from the customer's point of view, the reasons why they will buy. This is much more powerful selling than just hitting them with features and benefits. The difference can be illustrated by the following two statements.

> ''Won't the people in the warehouse prefer to keep the same shelf layout, even when the new system comes along?''
> ''If you buy the system I am selling, you will not have to change the shelf layout.''

The first is seeking to agree a criterion for, or a basis of, the decision. The second is simply a statement of a feature. As the campaign goes forward, the BoD changes, and this question keeps reminding the selling team that they need to make sure as far as they can that the current criteria suit their case. In the end, of course, the BoD which includes a feature or issue that is unique to one of the selling companies tilts the balance firmly in their favor.

IMPLEMENTABILITY

This word is coined to allow the selling team to assess how well they are organized to ensure an efficient implementation. It examines the resource requirements which will result in a successful project from both sides' point of view.

There are three subsidiary questions here:

» are the customer's implementation resources available and allocated to this project?
» do you have management agreement to the sales resources required to carry out the campaign plan?
» are the implementation support resources from your side identified and allocated?

Are the customer's implementation resources available and allocated to this project?

Once again, the professional solution-seller is being up-front with what the customer is going to have to do. A resource deficiency, or absence of know-how or skills, should be seen as offering an opportunity to the seller, rather than as a threat.

Do you have management agreement to the sales resources required to carry out the campaign plan?

At the first planning session, the answer to this will be "no." It is not until the team have presented the plan, and its resource implications, to management and got their agreement to their allocation that the answer to this question becomes affirmative.

Are the implementation support resources from your side identified and allocated?

If you are to be convincing in your presentation of how the project will succeed if the buyer says "yes," you need to know that support will be available at the time it is needed. The risk which your company will take by making this sale is, to a considerable extent, defined by understanding what support will be necessary and having a very good idea of where it will come from.

The answer to this question is rarely straightforward. Management are estimating resource requirements from a knowledge base which is inevitably incomplete. They are making their best estimates, not only of resource requirements but also of what projects and combinations of projects are actually going to be sold and implemented.

COMPETITIVE POSITION

All the qualification work which has gone before should allow the team to answer the crucial question of whether or not they are likely to win this business against the competition.

The biggest waste of any salesperson's time is the time they spend on bids and tenders which are then lost. Ultimately, qualification is about whether you are spending your own, and your team's, time wisely and whether that time could be more profitably used elsewhere.

There are two subsidiary questions:

» can you identify one or more areas where you have a competitive advantage?
» is there an acceptably small number of competitors bidding for this project?

Can you identify one or more areas where you have a competitive advantage?

Without this the team is selling purely on price. That is, if all other things are equal, the customer will choose the cheapest bid. This is an unacceptable situation and the selling team must try to establish some feature of their offering which distinguishes it from the competition's.

Risk is a good area. Look at your company, its experience, size, etc., and try to get the customer to understand how much more likely the project is to be successful if they go with you. Whatever the area, find your competitive edge, so that in the action plan stage of the campaign planning process you can work out how to exploit that edge.

Is there an acceptably small number of competitors bidding for this project?

Some buyers start off the market-testing and bidding process by inviting everyone who could possibly be involved to give information and presentations. There is a lot of risk in this for the selling teams, who could get too deeply embroiled in selling before the project has sufficient definition. They need to assess whether or not the project represents a good business opportunity for them. This question will make the team limit their effort and lay a plan to try as quickly as possible to get the competing teams whittled down to an acceptable level.

WORKED EXAMPLE – DRAWING THE "SPIDER'S WEB"

It is very useful to present the qualification checklist as a radar diagram which, because of its appearance, I call the "spider's web."

In time, planning teams will start to see patterns in their spider's webs that they can recognize. The spider's web can also be used as a presentation aid when describing the state of a sales campaign to a manager or other interested party. Some companies have adopted the spider's web into their culture – they have familiarized everyone with the concept so that there is a completely consistent approach to qualification and briefings. Figure 7.1 shows an example.

The following is a breakdown of the rationale behind the spider's web.

» **Customer need (score 7).** There is a good *prima facie* requirement which is agreed by the decision-maker to be strategically desirable. It will be well worth our effort. The only problem here is that we do not understand the process for deciding on RoI.

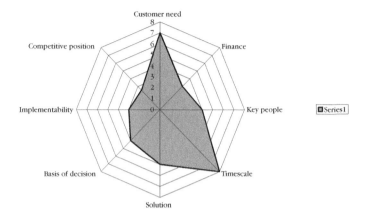

Fig. 7.1 Radar diagram or "spider's web."

» **Finance (score 3).** The decision-maker has said that they will make the money available, if their people put forward a business case. It is not yet in a budget.

» **Key people (score 4).** We know who the key people are, but have no further access to the decision-maker until the time of proposal. The technical recommender, who is taking the lead, is trying to block us from the user-recommenders.

» **Timescale (score 8).** Good news here, as the timescale is driven by a product launch which the customer is planning as a key date. The pressure on the launch date results from new legislation, so it is highly unlikely to be postponed.

» **Solution (score 5).** We have done this sort of thing many times before, but we are going to have to work with a third party with whom we have had no prior dealings. Once we agree the way ahead with the third party, the situation should improve.

» **Basis of decision (score 4).** We do not know the financial basis of decision. The technical basis is clear but contains no unique reason why they should buy from us. Our lack of contact with the user-recommenders means that we do not understand the practical issues to be covered.

» **Implementability (score 3).** It is a bit early in the campaign to be able to allocate resources. On the face of it, though, it does not look too difficult.

» **Competitive position (score 2.5).** There are four competitors bidding and we have no reason to think that we are better or worse placed than any other. (In Chapter 10 there is a step-by-step guide on how to move the opening position forward by working in a systematic way with the key people until the team get themselves into a winning position.)

KEY LEARNING POINT

Since the situation that the customer is in changes over the time of a sales campaign, the qualification process never stops. Indeed, qualifying the prospect and using the spider's web can be an excellent way for the salesperson and their manager to monitor the success of the campaign, warn of possible dangers emerging, and ensure that the team are making progress at the planned rate. If you have to pick one element of qualification as the most crucial, it would be the questions concerning the key people on the buyer's side. For example, if you are not talking to at least the same level of contact within the customer organization as the competition is, your campaign is taking a great (and probably unnecessary) risk.

Key Concepts

and Thinkers

This chapter describes, in a glossary of terms, some key words and concepts in selling and account management, and considers some words of wisdom from key thinkers in sales and consultative selling.

Some people regard the expression "solution selling" as a paradox. A solution, they argue, is an answer to a requirement, while selling is persuading people to do something they initially do not want to do. It is true that most people do not enjoy being "sold to," however much, in some circumstances, they may also enjoy making decisions and buying things. I think it is the processes of solution selling that defy the paradox. A professional salesperson, by taking a prospect through a logical buying process and running their campaign by the rules of a professional selling process, may very well arrive at a buying conclusion that the prospect did not desire or expect at the start of the two processes. That, if you like, is the salesperson's contribution – they make things happen that would otherwise not have.

Any experienced salesperson or sales manager, when asked the question, "What is the most important attribute of a professional salesperson?" will answer, "The ability to listen actively." Not, as many non-salespeople might think, "The ability to talk and argue persuasively." Indeed, I recently had dealings with an estate agent who bombarded me with arguments as to why I should stay in a particular property deal. He did this so much that eventually I positively discriminated against any advice he gave me and wanted to have the pleasure of telling him that I would never buy anything from him. And yet, intuitively, this person looks and sounds like a salesperson, and I formed a very favorable first impression.

SHIPLEY LTD – SOLUTION SELLING®

To illustrate, consider how the above issue is addressed by the UK-based business development specialists, Shipley Ltd., who have developed a training program known as "Solution Selling®." The following statement, taken from their Website (http://www.shipleylimited.com/SS.htm) encapsulates their approach.

> "The primary objective in Solution Selling® is to teach 'Journeymen' sellers to consciously emulate the behaviour of the intuitive natural sellers [who] Solution Selling® refers to as 'Eagles.' Feedback from those companies whose sales staff have been trained in the Solution Selling® process have found that a

Journeyman seller executing the right process can beat the Eagle seller who is 'winging it.'

"Most people readily agree that they love to buy things, but hate to feel 'sold to.' Most people have had unpleasant experiences with sellers where they have come away feeling taken advantage of, manipulated or coerced into doing something they really didn't want to do. If you carefully observe Eagles, you will realize they have conversations with their prospects. They don't make presentations. It takes far more knowledge and skill to have an intelligent conversation with someone than it does to present to him/her."

My estate agent was definitely not an Eagle!

MACK HANAN – CONSULTATIVE SELLING

Many salespeople assure their prospects and customers that if they buy from them they will be investing in not just a supplier of goods and services, but also a partner for their operation. Many assure, but few actually deliver on this promise. Indeed, if you probe them, few can actually define what a partnership between a customer and a supplier is.

Mack Hanan's book, *Consultative Selling* (Amacom, 1995), gives as good a definition of the processes involved in becoming your customer's partner as you can get. His starting point is this:

"Consultative selling is profit-improvement selling. It is selling to high-level customer decision-makers who are concerned with profit – indeed who are responsible for it, measured by it, evaluated by it and accountable for it."

The process involves analyzing trends in the customer's product and markets, researching the customer's business, developing customer strategies for growth, and finally recommending actions that the customer should take to improve their profits. If you do this, Hanan maintains, you will be pretty much immune from competitors because you are offering a much more valuable kind of service. In fact, the supplier is more or less going through the same process as the customer.

The consultative selling process includes becoming involved in the customer's evaluation of your proposition from a return-on-investment perspective. Hanan says that an opportunity window opens for the salesperson when the following conditions are met:

» the dollar value of the profits from your solution exceed's the dollar value of the customer's problem;
» the dollar value of the profits from your solution exceed's the dollar value of the costs of your solution; and
» the dollar value of the profits from your solution exceed's the dollar value of the profits from competitive solutions.

In order to know this, the salesperson has to be privy to the customer's process of investment appraisal and purchasing, with an emphasis on the financial side, and be able to assist the customer to estimate the benefits of the solution. It is not easy to get into that position with a customer – it requires a high level of contact and an even higher level of confidence in the account manager and their integrity. But it can be done, as long as the salespeople can ask the right questions and use their (or their finance people's) knowledge to assist the customer in this way.

As long as the average salesperson still imagines that their greatest skill is to describe the features of their products and services in sometimes insufferable detail, professional salespeople who join in the debate about the way ahead for their customers with the senior managers they deal with have an immense competitive edge.

GLOSSARY

Account management – the ongoing strategic direction of major clients' business.

Benefits – those things that the service does for, or means to, buyers, rather than the factual descriptions of it (which are its "features" – see below).

Buying process – a step-by-step methodology by which a buyer examines proposed expenditure and makes a logical, as well as an emotional, decision.

Buying signals – signs that the buyer is at a stage of understanding and acceptance that permits an attempt at closing.

Call frequency – the number of times in a year a customer is scheduled to receive regular calls. Sometimes used to categorize customers and describe their relative importance.

Call plan – the statement of work to be done with customers, arranged with productivity and effectiveness in mind.

Client records – the base of information, from contact details to buying records, that can be consulted in planning the next action with existing and past clients.

Closing – action taken to gain a commitment to buy or proceed onwards towards the point where this can logically occur.

Cold-calling – approaches to potential customers by any method (face-to-face or telephone, say) where they are "cold" – i.e., have expressed no prior interest of any sort.

Competitor intelligence – the information collected about competitive products and services and their suppliers that may specifically be used to improve the approach taken on a call.

Cost justification – the part of the sales argument that deals directly with price, relating it to results or benefits, and describing value for money.

Cross-selling – the technique of selling across, ensuring that a range of different products or services are bought by a client who starts by buying only one.

Ego drive/empathy – Mayer and Goldberg's terms for, respectively: the internal motivational drive that makes the good salesperson *want* to succeed; and the ability to see things from other people's (i.e., customers') point of view and, importantly, being seen to be doing so.

Features – the factual things to be described about a service (and see "benefits" above).

Field training – simply training (or development) activity away from any formal setting, undertaken out and about on territory.

Gatekeeper – someone who, through their position, can facilitate or deny access to a potential buyer (e.g. a secretary).

Handling objections – the stage of the sales presentation which is most highly interactive and where specific queries (or challenges) posed by potential buyers must be addressed to keep the positive side of the case in the majority.

Influencers – people who, while not having exclusive authority to buy, influence the buyer (through, say, their recommendation).

Kerbside conference – the post-call "post mortem" and development session held when a sales manager is accompanying salespeople in the field (which may often take place in the car – hence the name).

Key/major/national accounts – a variety of names are used here. First, measures vary as to what a major customer is. Simplistically, it is only what an individual organization finds significant. A second significant factor is the lead-time involved. In industries selling, say, capital equipment, it may take many months from first meeting to contract, and there is an overlap here with "major accounts."

Need identification – the process of asking questions to discover exactly what clients want, and why, as a basis for deciding how to pitch the sales presentation.

Negotiation – a different, though closely allied, skill to selling and very important in some kinds of business (see the ExpressExec book *Negotiating* for a useful reference).

On-the-job training – field training and development activity, often starting with joint calls with a manager.

Petal system – a practical way of organizing journeys to minimize time and mileage and thus help maximize productivity.

Pie system – a structured way of managing the spread of customers and prospects around a sales territory.

Pitch – a formal presentation which is part of the sales process, which may be general or in response to a specific brief.

Proposal – normally implies a written document, one including the price, but more than a quotation. It spells out the case and most often reflects a clear brief which has been given or established.

Prospecting – the search for new contacts who may be potential clients, encompassing everything from cold-calling to desk research to identifying names.

Qualifying prospects – research or action to produce information to demonstrate that cold prospects are "warm" and that you are winning competitively.

Return on investment (RoI) – a logical process to compare the financial implications of one investment or expenditure with another.

Sales aids – anything used during the sales conversation to enhance what is said. They may include items, information (a graph, say), or even other people.

Sales audit – an occasional systematic review of all aspects of the sales activity and its management, to identify areas which need improvement, or which are working well but need extension. A process that recognizes the inherent dynamic nature of sales.

Sales campaign – the planning and execution of the selling process leading to winning a sale.

Sales plan – a documented list of the actions, along with a timescale and making someone responsible for each action, required to win a sales campaign.

Sales productivity – the sales equivalent of productivity in an area, the focus here is on efficiencies that maximize the amount of time spent with customers (rather than traveling, writing reports, etc.). It focuses on ratios and touches on anything that increases sales success, however measured.

Sales strategy – a statement of how and why a sales team is going to carry out and win a sales campaign.

Selling process – a logical set of steps that sales teams need to go through to win a sales campaign.

Spin – although a registered trademark of Huthwaite Research Group Ltd in the context of its SPIN® Selling, the ordinary English word "spin" is used generically to describe a customer-focused and questioning-based approach to identifying clients' needs and selling appropriately in light of that knowledge.

Stakeholder – anyone who is involved with a buying decision, even in a minor way.

Standards – pre-set targets (absolute, moving, or diagnostic standards are all employed) used to direct sales activity and to set objectives.

Team selling – selling in partnership with others together in the same meeting, who might be colleagues or collaborators.

Territory – the area covered by an individual salesperson. It usually, but not always, refers to a geographic area.

Resources

This chapter explains how the annual report of a key account can be used as a starting point and a basic resource document for planning a complex sales campaign, and looks at some Websites that offer electronic sales-planning tools.

WEBSITES

The Speaking Connection

www.speakingconnection.com/Seminars/Sales_seminar.html

This is a US company offering training for the complex sales planner. They are particularly interesting because their emphasis is on finding an individual company's differentiator. As they put it on their Website:

> "What Makes You Unique?
> "Customers are more fickle than ever. Products are looking more and more alike. Quality is now expected and no longer a competitive edge for products. How are you going to separate yourself and your company from the sea of sameness and close more sales? Try *Selling Solutions*.
>
> "This presentation deals with selling the solutions that you have to offer as opposed to the features of your product or service. The concentration on partnering with your client flies in the face of the traditional vending process. Learn how to increase margins by clearly defining your product or solution as a value-added solution to a specific problem, not simply playing the commodity game of offering more bells and whistles at the lowest price."

SofTools

www.SofTools.net

This is a Website describing a platform that a sales team can use for sales planning purposes. Because it is a Web-based system, teams can also use the platform to share techniques and learn from each other. It is described on their Website as follows:

> "... SofTools has created a web-based Integrated Performance Support System (iPSS) that enables business teams to consistently apply best-practice methods – such as business planning, risk management, or critical decision-making. The iPSS is seen as a 'Virtual Business Coach' in that it will:
>
> 1) teach the user about new techniques;
> 2) provide interactive templates for completing the task;

3) enable users to learn from each other and from the past;
4) give senior managers greater visibility and control across remote or virtual teams.

"In the current economic climate, iPSS are no longer optional for survival – they are a 'must-have.' By licensing the SofTools iPSS to leading training and consulting companies, our platform is used to address a variety of key issues currently facing modern businesses: 'how to make the salesforce more effective at planning campaigns,' 'how to monitor and control operational projects,' 'how to increase profit awareness at all levels of staff.' "

THE PROSPECT COMPANY'S ANNUAL REPORT

Salespeople sometimes underestimate the usefulness of the prospect's published annual report in planning a complex sale. Many experienced salespeople, however, justifiably use a quote from the customer's annual report to start off any presentation or proposal that they make. It must, after all, introduce the topic of the presentation in the light of the company's strategies or issues – not a bad starting point for a team trying to impress managers that their proposal has strategic fit.

Consider the "balanced scorecard" described by Kaplan and Norton:

» **customers** – how do they see us?
» **internal** – what must we excel at?
» **financial** – how do shareholders see us?
» **innovation** – how can we continue to learn, improve, and add value?

Used well, the annual report can give us answers to the Kaplan–Norton questions above. Some people, who are comfortable with the financial pages, tend to ignore the rest of the report. They argue that the other parts of the report are mere advertisements for the company and the brilliance of its directors, while the financial pages are regulated in such a way that they represent the truth about the company. Unfortunately, neither of these statements is entirely true. Companies do use "creative accounting," which sticks to the letter of the law, but nevertheless paints a picture that misleads rather than guides the reader. On the other hand, those who are less comfortable with the financial side try to make do with the other parts of the report to try to understand the company – but it is of little use to understand the directors' view of the forward strategy of the company if you cannot check that the company's financial situation will allow them to implement it. A company talking about, for example, growth by acquisition is less likely to succeed if financially it is already in a lot of debt. Shareholders in the acquisitive dot.com companies suffered badly from this, if they did not check just how huge the debt problem was becoming for the acquirer.

The contents of an annual report

The chairman and directors of a company use the annual report as an advertising document as well as the means to satisfy legal reporting requirements. They are unlikely to open with a sentence such as "We made a lot of mistakes this year and have to own up to a performance far below the potential of the business."

Scything through the propaganda is possible, however, for one very important reason. Unless engaged in actual fraud – fortunately a fairly remote possibility – they are bound to stick to the truth, albeit in its most acceptable form. The "spin" is always there, but in most cases a little detective work will reveal what the account team need to know.

Remember also that probably the key performance measure of a chairman is their ability to deliver to their business plan. This means announcing what the future of the business should be and then achieving it. This achievement of expectations is a principal concern of shareholders, who have set their own strategy in deciding on the type and qualities of the companies they want to buy into. The shareholders acknowledge, of course, that there is a risk that not all of these expectations will be delivered.

It is for this reason that you may from time to time hear of profit warnings emanating from your prospect. A chairman who realizes that the company is not going to be as profitable as they had led the shareholders and analysts to expect will tell them the moment the information is clear and the likelihood of underperforming is high. When this happens, God help the salesperson who ignores it – it will have an impact on their campaign soon enough.

This expectation is particularly important in the case of the dividend that shareholders have been led to anticipate from previous performance or from a statement of dividend strategy by the board. In order to meet expectations on dividends, the company has to deliver on expectations as to profit and cash. It needs the profit to cover the costs of the dividend and the requirements for the future of the business, and it needs the cash to actually pay out the dividend amounts. Shareholders will not take it in any other form and a bounced dividend check is highly unpopular! These drivers impact the company's strategy and therefore the strategy of the account team selling to it.

Mission statement

Many companies put their statement of intent, or their mission statement, on the front cover or in a key position on the first page. It is a key vision and strategy statement. They tend now to be getting shorter, and more useful. The salesperson should study it and use it to test the validity of what comes later. Every strategy statement and plan for the future should echo this mission statement, both in the annual report and, more importantly, in the sales plan.

Financial highlights

The inside cover and first page normally contain the company's view of the financial performance in the last year compared to the year before. This is interesting, but carefully prepared, so if you want a more independent and consistent way of looking at the financial progress of a company, you will need to use your own tool to make your own interpretation.

The chairman's statement

This is always a key description of the intentions of the company. It is impossible to predict what will be in any particular statement, except to say that the chairman will pick out the critical issues in the recent past and in the future. Often, these critical issues are what salespeople have to form an opinion on. They may well reveal opportunities for the selling team or threats that the current team plan will not work. The headings below are almost always covered in the chairman's statement.

» **Last year's financial performance.** Also as part of the historical performance, the chairman will normally comment on the main trading issues of the past year. They will put them into the context of the economic situation in the countries where the company mainly does business and will mention other factors outside the board's control which have had an impact, normally a negative impact, on the past year's performance.

» **Dividends.** In almost all cases, in the chairman's report you will see a statement that conveys the increase or decrease in dividend proposed for this year, which can be read as the board's strategy on dividend in the future.

» **The way ahead.** The chairman here picks out the vital issues involved in the next period of trading. Look carefully at this, as you are going to have to feel confident that the issue is in reality what will drive performance and that your sales plan for the prospect fits in. In most reports, the "prospects" section will reveal what the company believes is its main competitive advantage. If the salesperson can demonstrate that the products and services they are selling will assist this differentiation, then so much the better.

» **Structure and people**. At this stage in the statement, it is very likely that chairmen will comment on the company structure and the quality of the company's people – vital background information for the salesperson as they try to identify and understand the stakeholders and the key people.

Reports of the chief executive and directors

This report will contain a number of matters required by law. It may also include statements from the directors on the position of the company in a number of areas.

» **Principal activities.** This is, as it suggests, a short statement of the principal businesses in which the company operates.

» **Research and development.** Later in the notes to the accounts you will see the actual amount of money spent on this.

» **Directors.** At this point there is a series of items of information about the directors, their resigning by rotation, and their interests in the company's shares. In many reports, rather than having the

Table 9.1 The activity matrix.

Activity matrix	Market 1	Market 2	Market 3	Market 4	Market 5	Market 6	Market 7	Market 8
Product 1								
Product 2								
Product 3								
Product 4								
Product 5								

interests of the directors stated at this point, there is a reference to where this information can be found further into the report. This may very well help to determine where real power lies within the company.

» **Conclusion to the directors' report.** The company secretary, who generally has some legal training, signs the report. In larger companies, the secretary may very well be the most senior legal officer in the company, and an important source of information on the legal terms and conditions the company operates with its suppliers.

Review of operations

This is an important statement from which the selling team can derive the company's strategy. The detection of the overall strategy should not be too difficult to discern. After all, the board of a company is responsible for analyzing possible future plans, deciding on the appropriate strategy, and then communicating this to all the people who will be involved in its execution. Those involved in the execution are staff at all levels and in all functions. It is necessary to have a consistent pyramid of plans to ensure that what is happening on the shop floor and at the point of sale and delivery fits in with the plans of the directors. It is equally important that the plans of its suppliers also fit in, which is what makes the review of huge importance to the salesperson. This communication is very difficult to get right, and a failure in this respect is obvious to staff, shareholders, and customers alike.

The salesperson, however, needs a simple technique for detecting and documenting the board's strategy. The team should do this by means of the company activity matrix. The review of operations will contain in some form statements of the company's products and market segmentation, and we should be able to reproduce this in a simple matrix along the lines of Table 9.1 above. The harder the exercise is to do, the less well has the board explained itself to staff, shareholders, and customers.

Ten Steps to Winning Complex Sales Through People

People buy from people. The most important part of the complex selling process is dealing with the key people. Here are the ten steps necessary to do that:

» recognize the antagonistic;
» interest the indifferent;
» present to the aware;
» consult with the interested;
» demonstrate to those trying it out mentally;
» instruct the experimenter;
» support the committed;
» ally with the internalizer;
» identify the drivers and restrainers; and
» plan actions to move people up the chain.

One of the few certainties about a complex-buying decision is that it will change the jobs of quite a few people in the buying company if the sale is successful. Yet people are generally reluctant to change, and that reluctance can go through many stages, from belligerence to plain fear. It is the job of the selling team to get as many of the stakeholders as possible to go from whatever starting point they take to being, at best, enthusiastically committed to the project or, at worst, interested in looking further into the implications for them. The starting point is to correctly identify where the key people are on a scale of "attitude to change" and then work on improving that attitude to the best point possible.

WHAT IS THE ATTITUDE OF THE KEY PEOPLE?

In getting people to adopt your suggestions and proposals you have to be perceptive and methodical. My colleague John Wright, along with a behavioral psychologist, was responsible for the development of a planning strategy for selling to the key people based on the principle of change management.

As you consider the actions you need to take with each of the buyer's people, consider their starting point and attitude towards the change you are proposing. In your initial meeting with them they will reveal how they feel about the issue and how comfortable they will be about changing how they or their people do things.

Below, in summary, are the attitudes available to each of the key people.

» **Antagonistic** – for some reason they do not like even the thought of what you are proposing.
» **Indifferent** – they do not see at the moment what is in it for them, or are unaware that there will be an impact on them.
» **Aware** – they know of the proposal but have little knowledge about its impact on them.
» **Interested** – they have got to the stage of weighing up the matter and considering it a possibility.
» **Trying-out mentally** – this is a very good sign. It means that they are trying to work out how things will be for them if the proposal

were to win support. Perhaps the most famous example of trying-out mentally is the couple considering buying a house – when they discuss where they would put different pieces of furniture, they are at this stage.

» **Trying** – they are simulating the proposal in their own environment.

» **Committed** – the stage to which you are trying to get as many of the key people as possible, as quickly as possible. Once you reach a moment in time when they are all committed, ask for the order.

» **Internalizing** – denotes the time when the buyers have accepted the change and the new situation is now the norm.

As we move towards the tenth step in this chapter – action planning – the tables below should help you to decide which category the various key people are in and therefore the approach that you should take. Let this adoption strategy be your guide and consider at least those actions relevant to the stage your buyer is at.

Without a systematic approach, salespeople are likely to try to jump several steps at the same time. The theory of change management has proved that this does not work. Yet, how many times do salespeople work on people who are antagonistic, by demonstrating the products and services they are trying to sell? As you will see below, this is using the strategy and actions appropriate to a person at step five in the chain. An antagonistic person attending a demonstration will find exactly the faults and flaws of your proposition that they suspected, or at least try very hard to do so.

Taking this common mistake one stage further, you find salespeople giving demonstrations to a number of people. Suppose that one person in a group is at step seven (committed) and that you have invited them to attend a demonstration to a person known to be indifferent. If the person who is indifferent is senior to the other person, you may well bring the committed person back some steps as they witness how difficult it might be to get their boss to be enthusiastic about the proposal.

Let us go through the 10 steps and consider the implications of the key people at different stages on your chances of winning the order. The tables are a short summary of the tell-tale signs that reveal the type of person you encounter at each step, what your overall role with that person should be, and a few suggestions that have been successfully employed by salespeople in the past to move them on to the next step.

1. RECOGNIZE THE ANTAGONISTIC

Someone who is against your proposal will say and do anything to damage your case. Do some research to find out if, for example, your company has had any dealings with the person before. If they have, expect them to bring up anything that went badly during those earlier dealings. If the antagonism is present at the top of the buying organization, you may want to reconsider whether you are selling in the right place. (See Table 10.1.)

2. INTEREST THE INDIFFERENT

Some key people may not be involved in the early stages of the campaign and will not know what is going on. These people are frequently those who the buying organization's managers believe will have to live with the situation when the decision is made. Be careful about simply accepting this. People brought into what is more or less a

Table 10.1 Recognize the antagonistic.

Signs	Your role	Possible actions
Rude; irrational; finds many objections; no time for you. "We already do something like it." "Yes, but . . . " "You would say that, you are a salesman."	Be pleasant and tolerant. Bide your time to scatter seed corn. Use the weight of more senior people in the organization who are steps ahead, but beware of reinforcing prejudices against people they don't like.	Be welcoming; smile; talk about their interests; go at their pace; use their names frequently. Reduce any perceived threat, perhaps by reference to other people who have been in a similar situation. Probe for any fears or anxieties and work out how to remove them.

Table 10.2   Interest the indifferent.

Signs	Your role	Possible actions
·Shows no real interest. Changes the subject. Introduces red herrings; fidgets.	Similar to above. Show that you care about them and their involvement in the buying process.	Approach and be approachable. Reward approximations to awareness and interest in the solution or related topics. Face-to-face is best here, but use of the telephone, letter, article, or Internet reference, followed up soon afterwards, can be useful. Do not neglect the use of recommenders or champions.

fait accompli can turn very antagonistic and could spoil the sale if they convince enough senior people that they are not going to co-operate. (See Table 10.2.)

3. PRESENT TO THE AWARE

Some stakeholders, whilst not indifferent, are merely aware of what is going on. If you leave them like this they will not progress to the next step without your active intervention. (See Table 10.3.)

4. CONSULT WITH THE INTERESTED

Some people when you meet them will display the signs of being interested in making the change and assisting the selling and buying teams in exploring options. Consult with, and listen to, them. Be careful, though, not to give false impressions or to set expectations higher than they should be. If, later on, they are disappointed, they may well go back a number of steps. It is much better to obey the

Table 10.3 Present to the aware.

Signs	Your role	Possible actions
Passive. Has little information. Does not look for information. Has no opinions.	Presenter, not a demonstrator. You should ask a lot of questions about how they do the relevant part of their job at the moment, so that when you do get to the demonstration you can show them what the change will involve.	Look for openings and established need. Listen for any expression of need. Obtain attention by appealing to these needs, keeping presentation of the solution brief and focused on them and that need. Use oral, written, and pictorial material for them to read or look at. Discuss with them later during a feedback session.

salesperson's mantra – underpromise and overperform. The general rule is to set expectations high enough to move them up a step, but no more. (See Table 10.4.)

5. DEMONSTRATE TO THOSE TRYING IT OUT MENTALLY

Contrary to a lot of people's opinions, often the most effective demonstrations (measured by seeing if the audience move up to the next step) are not the really flashy ones where someone shows the product or service being expertly used by an experienced person, but a demonstration where the audience are involved in a hands-on capacity as early as possible. Remember the objective at this step – it is not to make people aware of every feature of the product or every possible use of it, but to

Table 10.4   Consult with the interested.

Signs	Your role	Possible actions
Open mind. Seeks information. Begins to form opinions. Personal concerns and questions about how the innovation will affect them and their organization.	Counsellor/consultant.	Match need to solution. Match information and characteristics of solution to real needs and basis of decision. Involve them in discussing. Encourage ideas from them. Link with the job and environment. Identify personal concerns; "their win-situation"; answer questions and provide information.

get them to agree to being a pilot or a guinea pig in further demonstrations. I always remind myself that the most used exhibits in the Science Museum are the ones with buttons to press and lights to light up.

So ask people to demonstrate to themselves a small element of the product. Make sure it is a part that is very easy to use – you want them to succeed without needing to be bailed out by an expert. (See Table 10.5.)

6. INSTRUCT THE EXPERIMENTER

Pay a huge amount of attention to the first people at this stage, often the pilot group. Their feedback is vital, and if you listen well they will simply tell you how to sell the concept to other people in their organization. Contact them frequently, every day if that is appropriate. However, remember the negative side of this – if they eventually do not like what they are doing, they could blow the project out of the water. (See Table 10.6.)

Table 10.5 Demonstrate to those trying it out mentally.

Signs	Your role	Possible actions
Mentally tries out. Imagines in own situation. Expresses some views. Decides if worth trying.	Demonstrator.	Present and describe solution in more detail and sell benefits. Show how solution will work to provide benefits to buying company and people, including them. Give examples. Stimulate prospect to imagine the solution being used in their environment. Discuss.

Table 10.6 Instruct the experimenter.

Signs	Your role	Possible actions
Tries out, usually on a demonstration or pilot basis. Weighs evidence of trial.	Supporter and instructor.	Guide and support positive reactions. Handle objections, but show how you want to respond to suggestions and problems. Provide an actual trial demonstration. Guide them through it. Provide feedback and opportunities for talking to others who have benefited. Use reference-sells, by telephone or in person. Be around to handle any problems when the prospect is weighing the evidence.

7. SUPPORT THE COMMITTED

These people are your champions as you move towards the big decision. Cosset them, entertain them, take them to the opera or the Hard Rock Café if that is their thing. On the business side, keep in touch and don't assume that none of them will slip back steps by talking to people or seeing that some things are changing. (See Table 10.7.)

Table 10.7 Support the committed.

Signs	Your role	Possible actions
Accepts its worth and relevance; plans to use.	Supporter.	Support and maintain presence. Be around to prevent any event or person turning prospect against solution irrationally or inadvertently. Support and deal with difficulties professionally. If possible, manage the monitoring and evaluation. Reinforce and provide follow-up support.

8. ALLY WITH THE INTERNALIZER

Now you are back into prospecting mode. Where else can these people help you to get entry and start another complex sales campaign? (See Table 10.8.)

You have now taken the first view of the personal position of the buyers, and there is one other clue that you need, which is the subject of step nine.

Table 10.8 Ally with the internalizer.

Signs	Your role	Possible actions
Becomes an enthusiastic user and supporter. Use of solution becomes everyday behavior. The win/win situation is recognized.	Ally.	Capitalize on relationship of ally. Look for further opportunities and build on success. Capitalize on the change, and possibly on the relationships that have been made.

9. IDENTIFY THE DRIVERS AND RESTRAINERS

Some people in the group will be driving the project positively. They may not yet be committed but they are pushing their colleagues to take the proposal seriously. Others will be restrainers – for whatever reason, they are holding back from supporting even the investigation of the relevance of the solution. If the selling team understand why people have adopted their stance as drivers or restrainers, then they can plan what needs to be done to improve the position.

This list of possible sources of driving and restraining forces will be useful and will prompt you to think of others. All of them could influence people in either direction. Previous experience can be a driving force if that experience was good, but it can be a blocking or restraining force if the experience was bad. Remember that working on reducing restraining forces will, on balance, pay off more than increasing the driving forces.

All or any of the following factors could amount to a driving or a restraining force in any given situation.

» Allegiance to other methods.
» Alternative experience.
» Attitude towards change.
» Autonomy.
» Autonomy between divisions.

» Cost.
» Customary practices.
» Enthusiasm.
» Freedom.
» Job security.
» Management support.
» Number or quality of allies.
» Organization.
» Policy.
» Previous experience.
» Resources.
» Reward system.
» Self-development.
» Skill or capability of self or others.
» Social contacts.
» Status or authority.
» Time.
» Variety of work.
» Workload.

10. PLANNING THE SALES CALLS AND OTHER ACTIVITIES

When a salesperson and their team have now completed this systematic analysis of the key people in the campaign, it is time to start planning the actual activities. A benefit of good planning is that if the team have carried out the analysis phase well, the action plan and the milestones needed to achieve it will probably be fairly apparent. Often, the objectives or measures of actions can be stated as moving the person from one step in the change process to the next.

The team then assign the actions to individual members, who become responsible for that achievement within the timescale allowed. Members will have a lot of say on the timescale of their activities. After all, they have to fit them into their schedules and give the team a strong sense that the actions involved will be done and the people-objective achieved.

KEY LEARNING POINTS

» Getting all the key people onside and committed to the selling team's proposition forms the main aim of the team's action plan in a complex sale.

» If you add to your campaign the psychology involved in terms of people accepting change, you will take steps down the path of persuading people to accept your proposition at the right time. You will also go one step at a time, not expecting people to leap to accept change without going through the psychological process in a well-known and understood fashion.

» In some ways, adhering to this method of selling is aimed at avoiding making mistakes and antagonizing people, as much as it is aimed at moving people positively forward.

Frequently Asked Questions (FAQs)

Q1: How do you define a complex sale?

A: Complex sales require a *team* on both the seller's and the buyer's side. On the seller's side, they emphasize the need for an agreed strategy and sales plan so that everyone is concentrating their efforts on the strategy that the salespeople believe will win the business. See Chapter 2.

Q2: Should a complex sale be a profit-center?

A: It is advisable to have the profit element of a complex sale as part of the measure of performance of the salesperson. See Chapter 3.

Q3: What do you do if someone in the buying team is interested in what you are proposing?

A: Some people, when you meet them, will display the signs of being interested in making the change and assisting the selling and buying teams in exploring options. Consult and listen to them. See Chapter 10.

Q4: How long should a team spend on understanding the current situation before deciding on an action plan?

A: In general, the environmental analysis part of planning lasts three times as long as the action-planning part. See Chapter 6.

Q5: How do I give all the stakeholders access to my campaign plan?

A: Use a consistent Internet or intranet template and give the stakeholders appropriate permissions to see the complete plan. See Chapter 5.

Q6: What is the most effective way of getting sales-people to learn from each other?

A: Use a blended solution of limited face-to-face training, enhanced with online coaching and electronic tools. See Chapter 4.

Q7: Is there a quick way of measuring your position in a complex sale?

A: Use a radar diagram (or "spider's web") to measure yourself against the key attributes of a winning campaign. See Chapter 7.

Q8: What is a sales strategy?

A: A statement of how and why a sales team is going to carry out and win a sales campaign. See Chapter 8.

Q9: Does a key account's annual report give a sales team useful information?

A: Yes, in terms of the prospect's strategy, key issues, and financial health. See Chapter 9.

Q10: Is there a test to see if a prospect's requirement is a real need?

A: The best test is to ask whether, if you, the selling team, were running your customer's business, you would buy this product and go into this new environment See Chapter 7.

Index

EXPRESSEXEC –
BUSINESS THINKING AT YOUR FINGERTIPS

ExpressExec is a 12-module resource with 10 titles in each module. Combined they form a complete resource of current business practice. Each title enables the reader to quickly understand the key concepts and models driving management thinking today.

Available from:
www.expressexec.com

Customer Service Department
John Wiley & Sons Ltd
Southern Cross Trading Estate
1 Oldlands Way, Bognor Regis
West Sussex, PO22 9SA
Tel: +44(0)1243 843 294
Fax: +44(0)1243 843 303
Email: cs-books@wiley.co.uk

Printed and bound in the UK by
CPI Antony Rowe, Eastbourne

Printed and bound by CPI Group (UK) Ltd, Croydon, CR0 4YY

02/10/2023

08124242-0001